FAVORITE BRAND NAME
APPETIZERS, SALADS & SIDES

Publications International, Ltd.

Pictured on the front cover: Grilled Chicken Caesar Salad *(page 278).*

Microwave Cooking: Microwave ovens vary in wattage. Use the
cooking times as guidelines and check for doneness before adding
more time.

FAVORITE BRAND NAME

APPETIZERS, SALADS & SIDES

Dazzling

DRINKS

A.1.® Virgin Mary

- **2   cups tomato juice**
- **3   tablespoons A.1.® Steak Sauce**
- **¼   to ½ teaspoon liquid hot pepper seasoning (optional)**
-     **Ice cubes**
- **4   lime or lemon wedges, for garnish**
- **4   celery stalks, for garnish**

In small pitcher, blend tomato juice, steak sauce and hot pepper seasoning. Pour into 4 ice-filled 8-ounce glasses. Garnish with lime or lemon wedges and celery stalks. Serve immediately.   *Makes 4 servings*

Banana-Pineapple Colada

- **½   ripe banana, peeled**
- **½   cup fresh or canned pineapple chunks**
- **½   cup pineapple juice**
- **½   cup ice cubes**
- **1   tablespoon sugar**
- **¼   teaspoon coconut extract**

Place all ingredients in blender or food processor; process until blended thoroughly. Serve immediately.
Makes 2 servings

Favorite recipe from **The Sugar Association, Inc.**

Fuzzy Banana Navel

2 medium, ripe DOLE® Bananas,
    quartered
1 pint orange sorbet *or* 2 cups orange
    sherbet, slightly softened
1 cup DOLE® Mandarin Tangerine Juice

• Combine bananas, sorbet and juice in blender or food processor container. Blend until thick and smooth. Garnish with orange slices and curls, if desired. Serve immediately.   *Makes 4 servings*

Fuzzy Peach Navel: Substitute DOLE® Orchard Peach Juice for Mandarin Tangerine Juice.

Bronze Nectarine Margaritas

10   **Frozen California Nectarine Cubes (recipe follows)**
¾   **cup orange juice**
2   **tablespoons lime juice**
2   **tablespoons sugar**
10   **ice cubes, cracked**

Combine all ingredients in blender or food processor; process until smooth. Pour into stemmed glasses.

Makes 2 servings

Frozen California Nectarine Cubes: Slice 4 fresh nectarines. Combine in blender or food processor with 1/4 cup lime juice; process. Pour into ice cube trays; freeze. Makes 20 cubes.

Favorite recipe from **California Tree Fruit Agreement**

Margaritas, Albuquerque Style

1 lime, cut into wedges
  Coarse salt
1 can (6 ounces) frozen lime concentrate
¾ cup tequila
6 tablespoons triple sec
1 can (12 ounces) lemon-lime or
  grapefruit soda
3 to 4 cups ice cubes
  Lime twists, for garnish
  Lime peels, for garnish

Rub rim of each cocktail glass with lime wedge; swirl glass in salt to coat rim. Combine half of each of remaining ingredients, except garnishes, in blender; process until ice is finely chopped and mixture is slushy. Pour into salt-rimmed glasses. Repeat with remaining ingredients. Garnish if desired.

Makes 7 to 8 servings

Frozen Virgin Daiquiris

1 can (12 ounces) frozen DOLE® Pine-
   Passion-Banana Juice Concentrate or
   Pineapple Juice Concentrate, divided
3 cups water, divided
1 teaspoon rum extract (optional),
   divided
4 cups ice cubes, divided

• **Place** half of frozen juice concentrate, water, rum
extract and ice cubes in blender or food processor
container. Blend until mixture is slushy.

• **Pour** into tall glasses or large pitcher; set aside.

• **Repeat** blending with remaining ingredients.

• **Stir** before serving. Serve immediately.

Makes 10 servings

Cappuccino Cooler

1½ cups cold coffee
1½ cups chocolate ice cream
¼ cup HERSHEY᾿S Syrup
   Crushed ice
   Whipped cream

In blender container, combine coffee, ice cream and syrup. Cover; blend until smooth. Serve immediately over crushed ice. Garnish with whipped cream.
Makes about 4 (6-ounce) servings

Variation: Substitute vanilla ice cream for chocolate; increase syrup to ⅓ cup.

Iced French Roast

2 cups strong brewed French roast
    coffee, chilled
2 teaspoons sugar
½ teaspoon unsweetened cocoa powder
2 tablespoons low-fat milk
   Dash ground cinnamon

Place all ingredients in blender; process until combined. Pour over ice and serve immediately.
Makes 2 servings

Favorite recipe from **The Sugar Association, Inc.**

Viennese Coffee

1 **cup whipping cream, divided**
1 **teaspoon powdered sugar**
1 **bar (3 ounces) bittersweet or semi-
  sweet chocolate**
3 **cups strong freshly brewed hot coffee**
¼ **cup creme de cacao or Irish cream
  liqueur (optional)**
  **Reserved chocolate shavings, for
  garnish**

1. Place ⅔ cup whipping cream and sugar into chilled
bowl. Beat with electric mixer at high speed until soft
peaks form. *Do not overbeat.* Cover; refrigerate up to
8 hours.

2. Shave just enough chocolate for garnish; set aside.
Break remaining chocolate into pieces.

3. Place remaining ⅓ cup whipping cream in heavy,
medium saucepan. Bring to a simmer over medium-low
heat. Add chocolate pieces; cover and remove from
heat. Let stand 5 minutes or until chocolate is melted;
stir until smooth.

4. Add hot coffee to chocolate mixture, stirring until
heated through. Remove from heat; stir in creme de
cacao.

5. Pour into 4 warmed mugs. Top with whipped cream.
Garnish with chocolate shavings.

Makes 4 servings (about 3½ cups)

Coconut Snowball Cocoa

1 **pint vanilla ice cream**
1 **cup flaked coconut**
½ **cup unsweetened cocoa powder**
1 **quart milk**
½ **cup dark rum (optional)**
¾ **to 1 cup cream of coconut**
1 **teaspoon coconut extract**
½ **cup chocolate-flavored ice cream sauce (optional)**
8 **maraschino cherries (optional)**

Scoop ice cream into 8 small balls; immediately roll in coconut. Place on waxed-paper-lined baking sheet; freeze until ready to use. Whisk cocoa into milk in large saucepan. Stir in rum, if desired, cream of coconut and coconut extract. Bring to a simmer over medium-high heat. Pour into 8 large heat-proof mugs. Float ice cream balls in cocoa. Drizzle each ice cream ball with chocolate sauce and top with cherry, if desired. *Makes 8 servings*

Hot Spiced Cider

2 quarts apple cider
⅔ cup KARO® Light or Dark Corn Syrup
3 cinnamon sticks
½ teaspoon whole cloves
1 lemon, sliced
   Cinnamon sticks and lemon slices
      (optional)

1. In medium saucepan combine cider, corn syrup, cinnamon sticks, cloves and lemon slices. Bring to boil over medium-high heat. Reduce heat; simmer 15 minutes. Remove spices.

2. If desired, garnish each serving with cinnamon stick and lemon slice.

Makes about 10 (6-ounce) servings

Kahlúa® Brave Bull

1½ ounces KAHLÚA® Liqueur
1½ ounces SANZA® Tequila
   Lemon twist, for garnish

Pour Kahlúa® and tequila over ice in glass. Stir. Garnish with lemon twist. *Makes 1 serving*

Piña Colada Punch

3 cups water
10 whole cloves
4 cardamom pods
2 sticks cinnamon
1 can (12 ounces) frozen pineapple juice
    concentrate, thawed
1 pint low-fat piña colada frozen yogurt,
    softened*
1¼ cups lemon seltzer water
1¼ teaspoons rum extract
¾ teaspoon coconut extract (optional)
    Mint springs, for garnish

1. Combine water, cloves, cardamom and cinnamon in small saucepan. Bring to a boil over high heat; reduce heat to low. Simmer, covered, 5 minutes; cool. Strain and discard spices.

2. Combine spiced water, pineapple juice concentrate and frozen yogurt in small punch bowl or pitcher. Stir until frozen yogurt is melted. Stir in seltzer water, rum extract and coconut extract, if desired. Garnish with mint sprigs.   *Makes 12 (4-ounce) servings*

*You may substitute pineapple sherbet for low-fat piña colada frozen yogurt. When using pineapple sherbet, use coconut extract for more authentic flavor.

Super Delicious Berry-aladous Punch

1 bottle (40 ounces) DOLE® Country
      Raspberry Juice or Mountain Cherry
      Juice, chilled
1 bottle (2 liter) ginger ale, chilled
1 package (10 to 12 ounces) frozen
      raspberries, partially thawed
1 package (10 to 12 ounces) frozen
      strawberries, partially thawed

• **Combine** juice, ginger ale, raspberries and
strawberries in large punch bowl. Serve.

Makes 16 servings

Raspberry Wine Punch

1   package (10 ounces) frozen red
    raspberries in syrup, thawed
1   bottle (750 mL) white zinfandel or
    blush wine
¼   cup raspberry-flavored liqueur
    Empty ½ gallon milk or juice carton
3   to 4 cups distilled water, divided
    Sprigs of pine
    Fresh cranberries
    Tinsel

Process raspberries with syrup in food processor or
blender until smooth; press through strainer,
discarding seeds. Combine wine, raspberry purée and
liqueur in pitcher; refrigerate until ready to serve.
Rinse out wine bottle and remove label.

Fully open top of carton. Place wine bottle in center of
carton. Tape bottle securely to carton so bottle will not
move when adding water. Pour 2 cups distilled water
into carton. Carefully push pine sprigs, cranberries and
tinsel into water between bottle and carton to form
decorative design. Add remaining water to almost fill
carton. Freeze until firm, 8 hours or overnight.

Just before serving, peel carton from ice block. Using
funnel, pour punch back into wine bottle. Wrap bottom
of ice block with white cotton napkin or towel to hold
while serving.   *Makes 8 servings*

Spiced Cranberry Punch

2   cups KARO® Light Corn Syrup
¼   cup water
6   cinnamon sticks
2   tablespoons whole cloves
½   teaspoon ground allspice
2   quarts cranberry juice cocktail, chilled
1   quart orange juice, chilled
1   can (46 ounces) pineapple juice, chilled
2   quarts ginger ale, chilled
½   cup lemon juice

1. In medium saucepan combine corn syrup, water, cinnamon sticks, cloves and allspice. Bring to boil over medium-high heat. Reduce heat; simmer 10 minutes.

2. Cover and refrigerate until thoroughly chilled; strain to remove spices.

3. Just before serving, combine spiced syrup, fruit juices, ginger ale and lemon juice.

Makes about 36 (6-ounce) servings

Kahlúa® Party Punch

2 cups (16 ounces) KAHLÚA® Liqueur
1 can (12 ounces) frozen apple juice
      concentrate, undiluted
½ cup (4 ounces) lemon juice
1 small ice chunk
1 bottle (25.4 ounces) sparkling apple
      juice
1 quart club soda or lemon-lime beverage
1 bottle (750 mL) dry champagne
      Thin lemon slices and small orange
      slices, for garnish

Chill all ingredients well. Combine Kahlúa®, apple
juice concentrate and lemon juice. Pour over small
chunk of ice in punch bowl. Add sparkling apple juice,
club soda and champagne; stir gently. Add lemon and
orange slices.

Makes 30 (½-cup) servings (about 1 gallon)

Notes: Kahlúa®, apple juice concentrate and lemon
juice may be mixed and refrigerated the day before.

Recipe may be increased without adjustment.

Champagne Punch

1 orange
1 lemon
¼ cup cranberry-flavored liqueur or
    cognac
¼ cup orange-flavored liqueur or triple sec
1 bottle (750 mL) pink or regular
    champagne or sparkling white wine,
    well chilled
    Fresh cranberries (optional)

Remove colored peel, not white pith, from orange and
lemon in long thin strips with citrus peeler. Refrigerate
orange and lemon for another use. Combine peels,
cranberry-flavored and orange-flavored liqueurs in
glass pitcher. Cover and refrigerate 2 to 6 hours.
Just before serving, tilt pitcher to one side and slowly
pour in champagne. Leave peels in pitcher for added
flavor. Place 1 cranberry in bottom of each champagne
glass, if desired. Pour punch into glasses. Garnish as
desired.   *Makes 6 to 8 servings (4 cups)*

Nonalcoholic Cranberry Punch: Pour 3 cups well-
chilled club soda into ⅔ cup (6 ounces) cranberry
cocktail concentrate, thawed.
                    Makes 6 servings (3½ cups)

Cranberry Pineapple Smoothie

- 2 cups Cranberry Pineapple Smoothie Base (recipe follows)
- 1 large ripe banana (optional)
- 4 cups ice cubes
  Orange peel and mint leaves (optional)

1. Prepare Cranberry Pineapple Smoothie Base.

2. In blender combine 2 cups Smoothie Base and banana; process until smooth. With blender running, add ice cubes, several at a time. Blend until thick and smooth.

3. If desired, garnish with orange peel and mint leaves.
Makes about 6 (6-ounce) servings

Cranberry Pineapple Smoothie Base

- 1 cup KARO® Light Corn Syrup
- 1 can (16 ounces) whole-berry cranberry sauce
- 1 can (8 ounces) crushed pineapple in unsweetened juice, undrained

1. In blender combine all ingredients; process until smooth.

2. Store covered in refrigerator up to 1 week.
Makes 4 cups base

Colada Smoothie

½ cup Piña Colada Smoothie Base (recipe
   follows)
1 small ripe banana
1 cup pineapple juice
4 cups ice cubes
¾ cup rum (optional)
   Fresh fruit (optional)

1. Prepare Piña Colada Smoothie Base.

2. In blender combine ½ cup Smoothie Base, banana
and pineapple juice; process until smooth. With
blender running, add ice cubes, several at a time, then
rum. Blend until thick and smooth.

3. If desired, garnish with fresh fruit.

Makes about 6 (6-ounce) servings

Piña Colada Smoothie Base

1 cup KARO® Light Corn Syrup
1 can (8 ounces) crushed pineapple in
   unsweetened juice, undrained
1 can (15 ounces) cream of coconut
¼ cup lime juice

1. In blender combine all ingredients; process until
smooth.

2. Store covered in refrigerator up to 1 week.

Makes 3½ cups base

Pineberry Smoothie

1 medium, ripe DOLE® Banana,
   quartered
1 cup DOLE® Pineapple Juice
½ cup vanilla or plain nonfat yogurt
½ cup fresh or frozen strawberries,
   raspberries or blueberries

• **Combine** banana, juice, yogurt and strawberries in blender or food processor container. Blend until thick and smooth. Garnish with additional strawberries, if desired. Serve immediately. *Makes 2 servings*

California Shake

¾ cup DOLE® Pitted Dates, halved
1 medium, ripe DOLE® Banana,
    quartered
1 cup fat-free or low-fat frozen vanilla
    yogurt, slightly softened
½ cup low-fat or nonfat milk

• **Combine** dates and banana in blender or food processor container. Blend until dates are finely chopped.

• **Add** yogurt and milk; blend until thick and smooth. Serve immediately. Garnish with banana slices, if desired.   *Makes 2 servings*

Toasted Almond Horchata

3½ cups water, divided
2 (3-inch) cinnamon sticks
1 cup uncooked instant rice
1 cup slivered almonds, toasted
3 cups cold water
¾ to 1 cup sugar
½ teaspoon vanilla
  Lime wedges, for garnish

Combine 3 cups water and cinnamon sticks in medium saucepan. Cover and bring to a boil over high heat. Reduce heat to medium-low. Simmer 15 minutes. Remove from heat; let cool. Measure cinnamon-water to equal 3 cups, adding additional hot water if needed. Place rice in food processor; process using on/off pulsing action 1 to 2 minutes or until rice is powdery. Add almonds; process until finely ground (mixture will begin to stick together). Remove rice mixture to medium bowl; stir in cinnamon-water. Let stand 1 hour or until mixture is thick and rice is soft. Remove cinnamon sticks; discard. Pour mixture into food processor. Add remaining ½ cup water; process 2 to 4 minutes or until creamy. Strain mixture through fine-meshed sieve or several layers of dampened cheesecloth into half-gallon pitcher. Stir in 3 cups cold water, sugar and vanilla until sugar is completely dissolved. To serve, pour over ice cubes, if desired. Garnish, if desired. *Makes 8 to 10 servings*

Dole® Juice Spritzer

½ cup DOLE® Country Raspberry Juice or
    other DOLE® Juice
½ cup mineral or sparkling water

• Pour juice and mineral water over ice cubes in large
glass. Garnish with lime wedge and citrus curl, if
desired.   *Makes 1 serving*

Fruity Spritzer

1 teaspoon strawberry extract
2 sugar cubes
1 cup chilled seltzer water

Place strawberry extract in small bowl; add sugar cubes
and let stand 5 minutes. Place flavored sugar cubes in
bottom of glass and add seltzer. Let cubes dissolve;
serve immediately.   *Makes 1 serving*

Favorite recipe from **The Sugar Association, Inc.**

Old-Fashioned Lemonade

LEMONADE SYRUP
- 2 lemons
- 2 cups KARO® Light Corn Syrup
- ½ cup water
- ⅛ teaspoon salt
- 1 cup fresh lemon juice

1. With sharp knife or vegetable peeler remove large strips of peel from lemons, being careful **not** to include any white.

2. In medium saucepan stir lemon peel, corn syrup, water and salt. Bring to boil over medium-high heat; boil 5 minutes. Remove from heat. Stir in lemon juice. Remove lemon peels.

3. Store covered in refrigerator up to 10 days.

Makes 4 cups syrup

To make Lemonade: In tall, ice-filled glass combine ½ cup Lemonade Syrup and ½ cup chilled water or club soda; stir to blend.

Real Old-Fashioned Lemonade

Juice of 6 SUNKIST® Lemons (1 cup)
¾ cup sugar (or to taste)
4 cups cold water
1 SUNKIST® Lemon, sliced crosswise
Ice cubes

In large pitcher, combine lemon juice and sugar; stir until sugar dissolves. Add remaining ingredients and blend well. Serve immediately.

Makes 6 (8-ounce) servings

Pink Lemonade: Add a few drops red food coloring or grenadine syrup.

Honeyed Lemonade: Add honey to taste in place of sugar.

Pineapple-Mint Lemonade

1   cup sugar
⅔ cup water*
1   can (46 ounces) DOLE® Pineapple
      Juice
1   cup lemon juice
⅓ cup chopped fresh mint

• **Combin**e sugar and water in large saucepan; bring to boil. Boil 1 minute; remove from heat.

• **Stir** in pineapple juice, lemon juice and mint; let stand 15 minutes.

• **Strain** lemonade into large pitcher; discard mint. Serve over ice cubes in tall glasses. Garnish with fresh mint sprigs, if desired.   *Makes 8 servings*

*For less tart lemonade, use 1 cup water instead of ⅔ cup.

Summer Spritzer: Combine 2 cups Pineapple-Mint Lemonade with 2 cups mineral or sparkling water. Serve over ice.   *Makes 4 servings*

Paradise Fruit Tea

1 bottle (40 ounces) DOLE® Orchard
   Peach Juice or Tropical Fruit Juice
1 cinnamon stick, broken in half
4 orange-flavored herb tea bags

• **Combine** juice and cinnamon in large saucepan. Bring to boil; remove from heat.

• **Add** tea bags; let stand 10 minutes. Remove tea bags and cinnamon.

• **Serve** tea over ice cubes in tall glasses or chill in refrigerator in large pitcher. Garnish with orange slices, if desired. *Makes 5 servings*

Peach-Melon Cooler

3 cups cubed DOLE® Cantaloupe
5 cups DOLE® Orchard Peach Juice or
    Pineapple-Orange Juice, divided

• **Place** melon and 1 cup juice in blender or food processor container. Blend until smooth.

• **Combine** melon mixture and remaining juice in large pitcher. Chill 1 hour before serving. Stir before serving. Garnish with skewered fresh fruit, if desired.

Makes 7 servings

Sangría

1 cup KARO® Light Corn Syrup
2 lemons, sliced
1 orange, sliced
½ cup brandy
1 bottle (750 mL) dry red wine
2 tablespoons lemon juice
1 bottle (12 ounces) club soda or seltzer, chilled

1. In large pitcher combine corn syrup, lemon and orange slices and brandy. Let stand 20 to 30 minutes, stirring occasionally.

2. Stir in wine and lemon juice. Refrigerate.

3. Just before serving, add soda and ice cubes.

Makes about 6 (8-ounce) servings

Sangría Blush

1   cup orange juice
½   cup sugar
1   bottle (1.5 liters) white zinfandel wine
¼   cup lime or lemon juice
1   orange, thinly sliced and seeded
1   lime, thinly sliced and seeded
16 to 20 ice cubes

Combine orange juice and sugar in small saucepan. Cook over medium heat, stirring occasionally, until sugar is dissolved. Pour into 2-quart container with tight-fitting lid. Add wine, lime juice and sliced fruits. Cover; refrigerate 2 hours. Place ice cubes in small punch bowl or large pitcher. Pour wine mixture over ice.   *Makes 8 servings*

Sangrita

1   can (12 ounces) tomato juice
1½   cups orange juice
¼   cup lime or lemon juice
1   tablespoon finely minced onion
⅛   teaspoon salt
¼   teaspoon hot pepper sauce
    Ice cubes
4   small ribs celery with leafy tops

Combine juices, onion, salt and hot pepper sauce in
1-quart container with tight-fitting lid. Cover;
refrigerate 2 hours. Pour into 4 ice-filled glasses. Add
1 celery rib to each glass for stirrer.

Makes 4 servings

Sparkling White Sangría

1 cup KARO® Light Corn Syrup
1 orange, sliced
1 lemon, sliced
1 lime, sliced
½ cup orange-flavored liqueur
1 bottle (750 mL) dry white wine
2 tablespoons lemon juice
1 bottle (12 ounces) club soda or seltzer, chilled
Additional fresh fruit (optional)

1. In large pitcher combine corn syrup, orange, lemon and lime slices and liqueur. Let stand 20 to 30 minutes, stirring occasionally.

2. Stir in wine and lemon juice. Refrigerate.

3. Just before serving, add soda and ice cubes. If desired, garnish with additional fruit.

Makes about 6 (8-ounce) servings

Spiced Red Wine

Grape Ice Ring (recipe follows)
½ cup sugar
½ cup water
1 bottle (750 mL) Burgundy wine, chilled
2 cups white grape juice, chilled
1 cup peach schnapps, chilled

Prepare Grape Ice Ring. Combine sugar and water in small saucepan. Bring to a boil. Boil, stirring constantly, until sugar dissolves. Cool to room temperature. Cover; refrigerate about 2 hours or until chilled.

Combine wine, grape juice, schnapps and sugar syrup in punch bowl. Float Grape Ice Ring in punch.

Makes 14 servings

Grape Ice Ring

2 pounds assorted seedless grapes
   (Thompson, Red Empress, etc.)
   Lemon leaves* (optional)

Fill 4-cup ring mold with water to within ¾ inch of top. Freeze about 8 hours or until firm. Arrange clusters of grapes and leaves on ice; fill with water to top of mold. Freeze about 6 hours or until solid. To unmold, dip bottom of mold briefly in hot water.

*These nontoxic leaves are available in florist shops.

Delightful

DIPS

Five-Layered Mexican Dip

½ cup low fat sour cream
½ cup GUILTLESS GOURMET® Salsa
   (mild, medium or hot)
1 jar (12.5 ounces) GUILTLESS
   GOURMET® Bean Dip (Black or
   Pinto, mild or spicy)
2 cups shredded lettuce
½ cup chopped tomato
¼ cup (1 ounce) shredded sharp Cheddar
   cheese
   Chopped fresh cilantro and cilantro
   sprigs (optional)
1 large bag (7 ounces) GUILTLESS
   GOURMET® Baked Tortilla Chips
   (yellow, white or blue corn)

Mix together sour cream and salsa in small bowl.
Spread bean dip in shallow glass bowl. Top with sour
cream-salsa mixture, spreading to cover bean dip.* Just
before serving, top with lettuce, tomato and cheese.
Garnish with cilantro, if desired. Serve with tortilla
chips. *Makes 8 servings*

*Dip may be prepared to this point; covered and refrigerated up to 24
hours.

Spicy Taco Dip

1 **pound BOB EVANS FARMS® Italian Roll Sausage**
1 **(13-ounce) can refried beans**
1 **(8-ounce) jar medium salsa**
2 **cups (8 ounces) shredded Cheddar cheese**
2 **cups (8 ounces) shredded Monterey Jack cheese**
1 **(4-ounce) jar sliced black olives, drained**
1 **cup sliced green onions with tops**
2 **cups sour cream**
1 **(1-pound) bag tortilla chips**

Preheat oven to 350°F. Crumble sausage into medium skillet. Cook over medium heat until browned, stirring occasionally. Drain off any drippings.

Spread beans in ungreased ½-quart shallow baking dish, then top with sausage. Pour salsa over sausage; sprinkle with cheeses. Sprinkle olives and onions over top.

Bake 20 to 30 minutes or until heated through. Spread with sour cream while hot and serve with chips. Refrigerate leftovers; reheat in oven or microwave.

Makes 12 to 16 appetizer servings

Taco Dip

12   ounces cream cheese, softened
½   cup sour cream
2   teaspoons chili powder
1½   teaspoons ground cumin
⅛   teaspoon ground red pepper
½   cup salsa
2   cups shredded lettuce
1   cup (4 ounces) shredded Wisconsin
      Cheddar cheese
1   cup (4 ounces) shredded Wisconsin
      Monterey Jack cheese
½   cup diced plum tomatoes
½   cup ripe olive slices
⅓   cup green onion slices
¼   cup pimiento-stuffed green olives
      Tortilla chips and blue corn chips

Combine cream cheese, sour cream and seasonings;
mix until well blended. Blend in salsa. Line 10-inch
serving platter with shredded lettuce; spoon on cream
cheese mixture. Top with remaining ingredients. Serve
with tortilla chips.   *Makes 10 servings*

Favorite recipe from **Wisconsin Milk Marketing Board**

Tijuana Taco Dip

1   **can (16 ounces) refried beans**
1   **can (8 ounces) tomato sauce, divided**
1¼ **teaspoons TABASCO® pepper sauce,**
     divided
1   **large tomato, chopped**
¾   **cup (3 ounces) shredded Monterey Jack**
     cheese
¾   **pound ground beef**
2   **teaspoons chili powder**
1   **cup sliced ripe olives**
1   **cup (4 ounces) shredded Cheddar**
     cheese
1   **cup sour cream**
     Chopped green onions, chopped
     tomatoes, ripe olive slices and
     cilantro, for garnish
     Taco or tortilla chips

Preheat oven to 350°F. In medium bowl combine
refried beans, 3 tablespoons tomato sauce and
½ teaspoon TABASCO® sauce; mix well. Spread evenly
in 1½-quart baking dish. Top with chopped tomato
and Monterey Jack cheese.

In large skillet cook beef and chili powder; stir
frequently until meat is browned. Remove from heat;
drain off fat. Stir in remaining tomato sauce, sliced
olives and remaining ¾ teaspoon TABASCO® sauce.
Spread evenly over Monterey Jack cheese. Sprinkle
with Cheddar cheese.

Bake 15 to 20 minutes or until cheeses melt and beans are hot. Remove from oven. Top with sour cream. Garnish with green onions, tomatoes, olives and cilantro. Serve warm with taco or tortilla chips.

Makes 12 appetizer servings

Black Bean Dip

1   can (15 ounces) black beans, rinsed, drained
½   cup **MIRACLE WHIP® FREE®** Nonfat Dressing
½   cup reduced-calorie sour cream
1   can (4 ounces) chopped green chilies, drained
2   tablespoons chopped cilantro
1   teaspoon chili powder
½   teaspoon garlic powder
    Few drops hot pepper sauce

Mash beans with fork in medium bowl. Stir in dressing, sour cream, green chilies, cilantro, chili powder, garlic powder and hot pepper sauce until well blended; refrigerate. Serve with tortilla chips.

Makes 2¼ cups dip

Tomato Salsa Pronto

1 can (14½ ounces) DEL MONTE®
  FreshCut™ Diced Tomatoes with
  Green Pepper & Onion
¼ cup finely chopped onion
2 tablespoons chopped cilantro
2 teaspoons lemon juice
1 small clove garlic, minced
⅛ teaspoon hot pepper sauce*
  Tortilla chips

Combine tomatoes, onion, cilantro, lemon juice, garlic
and hot pepper sauce. Add additional pepper sauce, if
desired. Serve with tortilla chips.

Makes 2 cups salsa

*Substitute minced jalapeño chile to taste for hot pepper sauce.

Chunky Salsa

2   tablespoons olive oil
1   cup coarsely chopped onion
1   cup coarsely diced green bell pepper
1   can (35 ounces) tomatoes, drained and
       coarsely chopped (reserve ½ cup
       juice)
1   tablespoon freshly squeezed lime juice
2   teaspoons TABASCO® pepper sauce
½   teaspoon salt
2   tablespoons chopped fresh cilantro or
       Italian parsley

Heat oil in large, heavy saucepan over high heat. Add
onion and bell pepper and sauté 5 to 6 minutes,
stirring frequently, until tender. Add tomatoes with
reserved ½ cup juice; bring to a boil over high heat.
Reduce heat to low and simmer 6 to 8 minutes, stirring
occasionally, until salsa is slightly thickened. Remove
from heat. Stir in lime juice, TABASCO® sauce to taste
and salt. Cool to lukewarm; stir in cilantro. Spoon salsa
into clean jars. Keep refrigerated up to 5 days.

Makes 3½ cups salsa

Fiery Guacamole Dip

- 2 **small ripe avocados**
- 3 **tablespoons FRANK'S® Original REDHOT® Cayenne Pepper Sauce**
- 3 **tablespoons minced cilantro**
- 3 **tablespoons lime or lemon juice**
- 1 **clove garlic, minced**
- ½ **teaspoon salt**
  Tortilla chips (optional)

Cut avocados in half crosswise; remove and discard pits. Scoop out flesh into medium bowl. Coarsely mash avocados. Stir in RedHot® sauce, cilantro, lime juice, garlic and salt; mix well. Cover and refrigerate until chilled or up to 3 hours. Serve with tortilla chips, if desired. *Makes 1½ cups dip*

Classic Guacamole

4   tablespoons finely chopped white onion,
      divided
1½   tablespoons coarsely chopped cilantro,
      divided
1   to 2 fresh serrano or jalapeño chilies,
      seeded, finely chopped
¼   teaspoon chopped garlic (optional)
2   large, soft-ripe avocados
1   medium very ripe tomato
      Boiling water
1   to 2 teaspoons fresh lime juice
¼   teaspoon salt
      Tortilla chips
      Chilies and cilantro sprig, for garnish

Combine 2 tablespoons onion, 1 tablespoon cilantro,
chilies and garlic in large bowl. Cut avocados lengthwise
in half; remove and discard pits. Scoop avocado flesh out
of shells; add to chili mixture. Mash roughly with wooden
spoon or potato masher, leaving avocado slightly chunky.

To loosen skin from tomato, place tomato in small
saucepan of boiling water 30 to 45 seconds. Rinse
immediately under cold running water. Peel tomato;
cut crosswise in half. Gently squeeze each half to
remove and discard seeds. Chop tomato.

Add tomato, lime juice, salt and remaining
2 tablespoons onion and ½ tablespoon cilantro to
avocado mixture; mix well. Serve immediately or cover
and refrigerate up to 4 hours. Serve with tortilla chips.
Garnish, if desired.   *Makes about 2 cups dip*

Green Pea Guacamole with Avocado and Tomato

½ cup diced ripe California avocado
3 tablespoons fresh lemon juice, divided
1 package (16 ounces) frozen petit peas, thawed
4 green onions
½ cup lightly packed fresh cilantro
1 jalapeño pepper, seeded
1 medium tomato, diced
    Reduced-fat tortilla chips (optional)

1. Combine avocado and 1 tablespoon lemon juice in medium bowl.

2. Combine peas, onions, cilantro, remaining 2 tablespoons lemon juice and jalapeño in food processor or blender; process until smooth. Add avocado mixture and tomato; gently stir to combine. Garnish with cilantro or tomato wedges and serve with tortilla chips, if desired. *Makes 8 servings*

Beefy Guacamole

1 pound ground beef
1 large onion, minced
1 package (1.0 ounces) LAWRY'S® Taco
   Spices & Seasonings
¾ cup water
1½ cups guacamole
2 medium tomatoes, chopped
1 cup (4 ounces) grated Cheddar cheese

In large skillet, brown ground beef and onion until beef is crumbly; drain fat. Add Spices & Seasonings for Tacos and water. Bring to a boil; reduce heat and simmer, uncovered, 10 minutes or until liquid is absorbed.

In small bowl, combine guacamole and tomatoes; blend well. In large bowl, layer half of beef mixture, guacamole mixture and cheese; repeat layers.

Makes about 4 cups dip

Festive Chicken Dip

1½ pounds boneless skinless chicken
    breasts, finely chopped
    (about 3 cups)
¼ cup lime juice, divided
2 garlic cloves, minced
1 teaspoon salt
½ teaspoon ground black pepper
1 can (16 ounces) refried beans
1½ cups sour cream, divided
1 package (1¼ ounces) dry taco seasoning
    mix, divided
1 tablespoon picante sauce
1 avocado, chopped
1 tablespoon olive oil
1 cup (4 ounces) shredded sharp Cheddar
    cheese
1 small onion, finely chopped
2 tomatoes, finely chopped
1 can (2¼ ounces) sliced black olives,
    drained and chopped
1 bag (10 ounces) tortilla chips
    Fresh cilantro, for garnish

Place chicken in small bowl. Sprinkle with 3
tablespoons lime juice, garlic, salt and pepper; mix
well. Set aside.

Combine beans, ½ cup sour cream, 2½ tablespoons taco
seasoning and picante sauce in medium bowl. Spread
bean mixture in bottom of shallow 2-quart casserole.

Combine avocado and remaining 1 tablespoon lime juice in small bowl; sprinkle over bean mixture. Combine remaining 1 cup sour cream and 2½ tablespoons taco seasoning in small bowl; set aside.

Heat oil in large skillet over high heat until hot; add chicken in single layer. Do not stir. Cook about 2 minutes or until chicken is brown on bottom. Turn chicken and cook until other side is brown and no liquid remains. Break chicken into separate pieces with fork. Layer chicken, sour cream mixture, cheese, onion and tomatoes over avocado mixture. Top with olives. Refrigerate until completely chilled. Serve with chips. Garnish with cilantro.   *Makes 8 cups dip*

Favorite recipe from **National Broiler Council**

Cucumber Dill Dip

1   package (8 ounces) light cream cheese,
    softened
1   cup HELLMANN'S® or BEST FOODS®
    Real or Light Mayonnaise or Low Fat
    Mayonnaise Dressing
2   medium cucumbers, peeled, seeded and
    chopped
2   tablespoons sliced green onions
1   tablespoon lemon juice
2   teaspoons snipped fresh dill *or*
    ½ teaspoon dried dill weed
½   teaspoon hot pepper sauce

1. In medium bowl beat cream cheese until smooth.
Stir in mayonnaise, cucumbers, green onions, lemon
juice, dill and hot pepper sauce.

2. Cover; chill to blend flavors.

3. Serve with fresh vegetables, crackers or chips.
Garnish as desired.   *Makes about 2½ cups dip*

French Onion Dip

1 container (16 ounces) sour cream
½ cup HELLMANN'S® or BEST FOODS®
    Real or Light Mayonnaise or Low Fat
    Mayonnaise Dressing
1 package (1.9 ounces) KNORR® French
    Onion Soup and Recipe Mix

1. In medium bowl combine sour cream, mayonnaise and soup mix.

2. Cover; chill to blend flavors.

3. Stir before serving. Accompany with fresh vegetables or potato chips. Garnish as desired.

Makes about 2½ cups dip

Fresh Garden Dip

1½ cups fat free or reduced fat mayonnaise
1½ cups finely shredded DOLE® Carrots
 1 cup finely chopped DOLE® Broccoli
     Florets
 ⅓ cup finely chopped DOLE® Green
     Onions
 2 teaspoons dill weed
 ¼ teaspoon garlic powder

• Stir together mayonnaise, carrots, broccoli, green onions, dill and garlic powder in medium bowl until blended.

• Spoon into serving bowl. Cover and chill 1 hour or overnight. Serve with DOLE® Broccoli Florets, Cauliflower Florets and Peeled Mini Carrots. Garnish with fresh dill sprigs, if desired. Refrigerate any leftover dip in airtight container up to 1 week.

Makes 14 servings

Smoky Eggplant Dip

1 large eggplant (about 1 pound)
¼ cup olive oil
3 tablespoons FRANK'S® Original
    REDHOT® Cayenne Pepper Sauce
2 tablespoons peanut butter or tahini
    paste
1 tablespoon lemon juice
2 cloves garlic, minced
¾ teaspoon salt
½ teaspoon ground cumin
    Spicy Pita Chips (recipe follows)

Place eggplant on oiled grid. Grill over high heat
15 minutes or until soft and skin is charred, turning
often. Remove from grill; let stand until cool enough to
handle.

Peel away charred skin with paring knife. Coarsely
chop eggplant. Place in strainer or kitchen towel. Press
out excess liquid. Place eggplant in food processor. Add
remaining ingredients except Spicy Pita Chips. Cover
and process until mixture is very smooth. Refrigerate
until chilled. Serve with Spicy Pita Chips.

Makes 1½ cups dip

Spicy Pita Chips: Split 4 pita bread rounds in half
lengthwise. Combine ½ cup olive oil, ¼ cup FRANK'S®
Original REDHOT® Cayenne Pepper Sauce and
1 tablespoon minced garlic in small bowl. Brush
mixture on both sides of pitas. Place pitas on grid. Grill
over medium coals about 5 minutes or until crispy,
turning once. Cut pitas into triangles.

Original Ranch Dip

- 2 cups (1 pint) sour cream
- ¼ cup mayonnaise
- 1 package (1 ounce) HIDDEN VALLEY RANCH® Milk Recipe Original Ranch® salad dressing mix

In medium bowl, whisk together all ingredients. Refrigerate at least 30 minutes before serving.

Makes about 2½ cups dip

Variations: Add any one of the following to prepared dip: 1 avocado, mashed, plus 1 teaspoon lemon juice and a dash of hot pepper sauce; ½ pared seeded cucumber, diced, plus ⅛ to ¼ teaspoon curry powder; ½ cup chopped shrimp or clams, plus 1 teaspoon lemon juice; 1 package (10 ounces) frozen spinach, thawed and squeezed dry, plus 1 tablespoon prepared mustard with horseradish.

Nutty Broccoli Spread

1 **box (10 ounces) BIRDS EYE® frozen Chopped Broccoli**
4 **ounces cream cheese**
¼ **cup grated Parmesan cheese**
1 **teaspoon dried basil leaves**
¼ **cup walnuts**
1 **loaf frozen garlic bread**

• Cook broccoli according to package directions; drain well.

• Preheat oven to 400°F. Place broccoli, cream cheese, Parmesan cheese and basil in food processor or blender; process until ingredients are mixed. (Do not overmix.) Add walnuts; process 3 to 5 seconds.

• Split garlic bread lengthwise. Spread broccoli mixture evenly over bread.

• Bake 10 to 15 minutes or until bread is toasted and broccoli mixture is heated through.

• Cut bread into bite-size pieces; serve hot.

Makes about 2 cups spread

Easy Italian Dip

1 container (16 ounces)
   BREAKSTONE'S® or KNUDSEN®
   Sour Cream
1 envelope GOOD SEASONS® Gourmet
   Parmesan Italian or Italian Salad
   Dressing Mix

Combine sour cream and salad dressing mix in
medium bowl. Refrigerate. Serve with bread sticks,
assorted cut-up vegetables or chips.

Makes 2 cups dip

Variations: Stir in any one of the following: ¼ cup sun-
dried tomatoes in olive oil, drained, chopped; ½ cup
roasted red pepper, chopped; 1 teaspoon roasted garlic
or 1 can (8½ ounces) artichoke hearts, drained, finely
chopped.

Spam™ Fiesta Dip

1 (15-ounce) can CHI–CHI'S® Refried
   Beans
1 (1¼-ounce) package taco seasoning
½ cup chopped green onions
1 (12-ounce) can SPAM® Luncheon Meat,
   cubed
1 (15-ounce) can HORMEL® Chili No
   Beans
1 cup (4 ounces) shredded Cheddar
   cheese
1 cup (4 ounces) shredded Monterey Jack
   cheese
1 cup sour cream
   Sliced ripe olives
   CHI–CHI'S® Salsa
   CHI–CHI'S® Tortilla Chips

Heat oven to 350°F. In small bowl, combine refried
beans and taco seasoning. Spread mixture on bottom of
12-inch pizza pan. Layer green onions, SPAM®, chili
and cheeses in pan. Bake 20 to 25 minutes or until hot
and cheeses are melted. Spread sour cream over top.
Sprinkle with olives. Serve with salsa and tortilla chips.

Makes about 24 appetizer servings

Party Cheese Wreath

2   packages (8 ounces *each*)
    PHILADELPHIA BRAND® FREE®
    Fat Free Cream Cheese, softened
1   package (8 ounces) KRAFT® FREE®
    Fat Free Shredded Natural Non-Fat
    Cheddar Cheese
1   tablespoon *each* chopped red bell
    pepper and finely chopped onion
2   teaspoons Worcestershire sauce
1   teaspoon lemon juice
    Dash ground red pepper

BEAT cream cheese with electric mixer on medium speed until smooth. Add cheddar cheese, mixing until blended.

ADD remaining ingredients; mix well. Refrigerate several hours or overnight.

PLACE drinking glass in center of serving platter. Drop round tablespoonfuls of mixture to form ring around glass, just touching outer edge of glass; smooth with spatula. Remove glass. Garnish with chopped fresh parsley and chopped red bell pepper. Serve with assorted fat-free crackers.   *Makes 2 cups spread*

Sun-Dried Tomato Cheese Ball

1 **package (8 ounces) cream cheese,* softened**
1 **cup (4 ounces) shredded Cheddar cheese**
⅓ **cup GREY POUPON® COUNTRY DIJON® Mustard**
1 **teaspoon dried basil leaves**
1 **clove garlic, crushed**
½ **teaspoon onion powder**
¼ **cup sun-dried tomatoes,** finely chopped**
⅓ **cup PLANTERS® Walnuts, toasted and chopped**
  Assorted crackers, bread sticks and bagel chips

In large bowl, with electric mixer at medium speed, mix cheeses, mustard, basil, garlic and onion powder until blended but not smooth. Stir in sun-dried tomatoes. Shape cheese mixture into 5-inch ball; wrap and chill 1 hour. Roll cheese ball in chopped nuts. Wrap and chill until serving time.

Serve as a spread with assorted crackers, bread sticks and bagel chips.   *Makes 1 (1-pound) cheese ball*

*Low-fat cream cheese may be substituted for regular cream cheese.

**If sun-dried tomatoes are very dry, soften in warm water for 15 minutes. Drain before using.

Pesto-Cheese Logs

⅓ cup walnuts, toasted
1 package (8 ounces) cream cheese, softened
⅓ cup refrigerated pesto sauce
2 ounces(about ⅓ cup) feta cheese, crumbled
2 teaspoons cracked black pepper
2 tablespoons finely shredded carrot
2 tablespoons chopped fresh parsley
  Assorted crackers
  Carrot slivers, parsley and fresh thyme, for garnish

1. Place walnuts in food processor; process until ground, but not pasty. Remove from processor; set aside.

2. Place cream cheese, pesto and feta in food processor; process until smooth.

3. Spread ¾ cup cheese mixture on sheet of waxed paper to form 4-inch-long log. Wrap waxed paper around cheese mixture. Repeat with remaining cheese mixture.

4. Refrigerate logs at least 4 hours or until well chilled. Roll each log back and forth to form 5-inch log.

5. Combine walnuts and pepper on sheet of waxed paper. Unwrap 1 log and roll it in walnut mixture to coat.

6. Combine carrot and parsley on another sheet of waxed paper. Unwrap remaining log and roll in carrot mixture to coat.

7. Serve immediately or wrap and refrigerate up to 1 day before serving. To serve, thinly slice log and serve with crackers. Garnish, if desired.   *Makes 2 logs*

Note: If you prefer, you may coat each log with ¼ cup chopped parsley instead of walnuts, pepper and carrot.

Hidden Valley Boursin Cheese

   2   **packages (8 ounces each) cream
         cheese, softened**
   ½   **cup butter or margarine, softened**
   1   **package (1 ounce) HIDDEN VALLEY
         RANCH® Milk Recipe Original
         Ranch® Salad Dressing Mix**
   1   **tablespoon Dijon mustard**
   1   **teaspoon minced garlic
         Round French bread**

In large bowl, beat all ingredients except bread with electric mixer until blended. Spoon into 3-cup serving bowl. Cover tightly and refrigerate overnight. Let stand at room temperature 30 minutes before serving.

To serve, slice off top of French bread. Remove inside, leaving ¼-inch-thick shell. Spoon cheese mixture into bread shell. Garnish with parsley and serve with additional French bread and vegetables, if desired.
                                                    Makes 2 cups dip

Pesto Cheesecake

CRUST

  1 cup fine dry bread crumbs
  ½ cup very finely chopped toasted pine
    nuts or walnuts
  3 tablespoons melted butter or margarine

FILLING

  2 cups (15 ounces) SARGENTO® Light
    Ricotta Cheese
  ½ cup half-and-half
  2 tablespoons all-purpose flour
  ½ teaspoon salt
  2 eggs
  ⅓ cup Homemade Pesto Sauce (recipe
    follows) or prepared pesto sauce

Preheat oven to 350°F. Lightly grease sides of 8-inch springform pan.

Combine bread crumbs, nuts and butter in small bowl until well blended. Press evenly onto bottom of pan. Refrigerate until ready to use.

Combine ricotta cheese, half-and-half, flour and salt in medium bowl with electric mixer. Beat at medium speed until smooth. Add eggs, one at a time; beat until smooth. Pour into prepared crust. Drop teaspoonfuls pesto over cheese mixture. Gently swirl with knife for marbled effect.

Bake 45 minutes or until center is just set; turn off oven. Cool in oven with door open 30 minutes. Remove from oven. Cool completely on wire rack. Cut into thin slices before serving.   *Makes 10 servings*

Homemade Pesto Sauce: In food processor or blender, process 1 clove garlic. Add ½ cup packed fresh basil leaves and 1 tablespoon toasted pine nuts or walnuts. Process until smooth, scraping down side of bowl once. With machine running, drizzle 2 tablespoons olive oil into bowl; process until smooth. Add ¼ cup (1 ounce) SARGENTO® Fancy Shredded Parmesan Cheese; process just until cheese is blended.

Hidden Valley Seafood Dip

1 cup cooked shrimp or crabmeat, finely
      chopped
1 cup (½ pint) sour cream
1 package (1 ounce) HIDDEN VALLEY
      RANCH® Milk Recipe Original
      Ranch® salad dressing mix
¼ cup chili sauce

In medium bowl, combine all ingredients; refrigerate at least 1 hour before serving. Serve with crackers or assorted vegetables for dipping.

Makes about 2 cups dip

Southwestern Seafood Dip

1 (15-ounce) can pinto beans, rinsed and
   drained
1 tablespoon plus 1 teaspoon taco
   seasoning mix
2 tablespoons fat-free sour cream
1 ripe avocado, coarsely chopped
1 tablespoon lime juice
1 tablespoon fat-free mayonnaise
¼ teaspoon Worcestershire sauce
⅛ teaspoon chili powder
⅛ teaspoon garlic powder
1 (8-ounce) package surimi seafood
3 tablespoons sliced ripe olives
½ small tomato, seeded and chopped
¼ cup corn
½ cup (2 ounces) shredded reduced-fat
   sharp Cheddar cheese
2 tablespoons chopped green onion tops

Mash beans with fork until almost smooth; stir in taco
seasoning mix and sour cream. Spread into 8-inch
circle on serving platter. Combine avocado, lime juice,
mayonnaise, Worcestershire, chili powder and garlic
powder. Mash with fork until well-blended; spread over
bean mixture. Shred surimi seafood with fingers;
sprinkle over avocado layer. Layer remaining
ingredients. Cover; refrigerate up to 2 hours. Remove
15 minutes before serving. Serve with tortilla chips.

Makes about 8 appetizer servings

Favorite recipe from **Surimi Seafood Education Center**

Salsa Shrimp Dip

1 **package (8 ounces) PHILADELPHIA BRAND® FREE® Fat Free Cream Cheese, softened**
½ **cup salsa**
1 **package (6 ounces) frozen cooked tiny shrimp, thawed (1½ cups)**

SPREAD cream cheese on serving plate. Top with salsa and shrimp. Serve with low-fat tortilla chips or assorted cut-up fresh vegetables.

Makes 1½ cups dip

Smoked Whitefish Spread

1 **package (8 ounces) PHILADELPHIA BRAND® FREE® Fat Free Cream Cheese, softened**
½ **pound smoked whitefish, skinned, boned, flaked**
2 **tablespoons finely chopped green onion**
1 **tablespoon chopped fresh dill**
1 **teaspoon lemon juice**
⅛ **to ¼ teaspoon black pepper**

BEAT cream cheese with electric mixer on medium speed until smooth.

ADD remaining ingredients, mixing until blended. Refrigerate until ready to serve. Serve with rye bread slices or assorted fat-free crackers. Garnish with lime wedges.

Makes 1½ cups

Smoked Salmon Spread

2 **packages (3 ounces each) cream
    cheese, softened**
3 **ounces smoked salmon, finely chopped**
1 **tablespoon chopped fresh dill or
    1 teaspoon dried dill weed**
2 **teaspoons lemon juice**
¼ **teaspoon hot pepper sauce**
¼ **cup HELLMANN'S® or BEST FOODS®
    Real or Light Mayonnaise or Low Fat
    Mayonnaise Dressing
    Belgian endive leaves
    Assorted party breads or crackers**

1. In medium bowl, beat cream cheese until smooth.
Stir in smoked salmon, dill, lemon juice and hot
pepper sauce until well mixed. Stir in mayonnaise until
blended. Cover; chill.

2. Spoon or pipe onto Belgian endive leaves or serve
with party breads or crackers. Garnish as desired.

Makes about 1¼ cups spread

Tuna Mushroom Paté with Orange Liqueur

 2 cloves garlic
 ½ medium white onion
 2 tablespoons butter
 1 jar (4½ ounces) sliced mushrooms,
      drained
 2 tablespoons orange liqueur or orange
      juice
 1 package (8 ounces) cream cheese,
      softened
 1 can (12 ounces) STARKIST® Solid
      White or Chunk Light Tuna, drained
 2 tablespoons fresh parsley leaves
 1 teaspoon grated orange peel
 ¼ teaspoon salt
 ¼ teaspoon coarsely ground black pepper
 ½ cup toasted slivered almonds (optional)
      Crackers or raw vegetables

In food processor bowl with metal blade, drop garlic
through feed tube while processing. Add onion; pulse
on and off to chop coarsely. In small skillet, melt butter
over medium heat. Add garlic and onion mixture; sauté
until onion is soft. Add mushrooms and liqueur; cook
until liquid evaporates. Cool.

In same food processor bowl with metal blade, place
cream cheese, tuna, parsley, orange peel, salt and
pepper. Pulse on and off to blend. Add cooled onion-
mushroom mixture; pulse on and off to blend. Stir in
almonds, if desired. Spoon into 1-quart serving bowl;
chill several hours or overnight. Serve with crackers.

Makes about 12 servings

Hot Clam Dip

1   package (8 ounces) PHILADELPHIA
      BRAND® Cream Cheese, softened
¼   cup milk
½   cup KRAFT® Real Mayonnaise
1   envelope GOOD SEASONS® Italian
      Salad Dressing Mix
2   cans (7½ ounces each) minced clams,
      drained
¾   cup chopped green, red and/or yellow
      pepper
½   cup (2 ounces) KRAFT® Natural
      Shredded Cheddar Cheese
¼   cup (1 ounce) KRAFT® 100% Grated
      Parmesan Cheese

HEAT oven to 375°F.

MIX cream cheese and milk in large bowl with wire
whisk until smooth. Stir in mayonnaise and salad
dressing mix until well blended.

STIR in clams, pepper and cheeses. Spoon into
1-quart baking dish.

BAKE 20 minutes or until heated through. Serve hot
with crackers, French bread slices or vegetable dippers.

Makes about 3½ cups dip

Hot Crabmeat Dijon Dip

- 1 **package (8 ounces) cream cheese,* softened**
- 6 **tablespoons GREY POUPON® Dijon Mustard, divided****
- ¼ **cup chili sauce**
- 2 **teaspoons prepared horseradish****
- 1 **teaspoon lemon juice**
- 1½ **teaspoons chopped fresh dill, divided**
- 1 **can (6 ounces) crabmeat, drained and flaked**
- ⅓ **cup plain dry bread crumbs**
- 1 **tablespoon margarine or butter, melted Vegetable crudités or assorted crackers, for dipping**

In medium bowl, with electric mixer at medium speed, blend cream cheese, 5 tablespoons mustard, chili sauce, horseradish, lemon juice and 1 teaspoon dill. Stir in crabmeat. Spoon mixture into greased 1-quart shallow baking dish. Combine bread crumbs, margarine or butter and remaining mustard and dill; sprinkle over crab mixture. Bake at 350°F for 20 to 25 minutes or until heated through. Serve with vegetable crudités or assorted crackers.

Makes 2 cups dip

*Low-fat cream cheese may be substituted for regular cream cheese.

**6 tablespoons GREY POUPON® Horseradish Mustard may be substituted for Dijon mustard; omit horseradish.

Hot Artichoke Dip

1 package (8 ounces) PHILADELPHIA
   BRAND® FREE® Fat Free Cream
   Cheese, softened
1 can (14 ounces) artichoke hearts,
   drained, chopped
½ cup (2 ounces) KRAFT® FREE® Nonfat
   Mayonnaise Dressing
½ cup KRAFT® FREE® Nonfat Grated
   Topping
2 tablespoons finely chopped fresh basil
   or 1 teaspoon dried basil leaves
2 tablespoons finely chopped red onion
1 clove garlic, minced
½ cup chopped tomato

BEAT cream cheese with electric mixer on medium
speed until smooth.

ADD all remaining ingredients except tomato, mixing
until blended. Spoon into 9-inch pie plate.

BAKE at 350°F for 25 minutes. Sprinkle with tomato.
Serve with assorted cut-up fresh vegetables or baked
pita bread wedges (recipe follows).

Makes 3¼ cups dip

Baked pita bread wedges: Cut 3 split pita breads
each into 8 triangles. Place on cookie sheet. Bake at
350°F for 10 to 12 minutes or until crisp.

Chunky Hawaiian Spread

1 package (3 ounces) light cream cheese,
    softened
½ cup fat free or light sour cream
1 can (8 ounces) DOLE® Crushed
    Pineapple, well drained
¼ cup mango chutney*

• **Beat** cream cheese, sour cream, pineapple and
chutney in medium bowl until blended.

• **Spoon** cream cheese mixture into medium serving
bowl. Cover and chill 1 hour or overnight. Serve with
low fat or fat free crackers. Refrigerate any leftover
spread in airtight container up to 1 week.

Makes 20 servings

*If there are large pieces of fruit in chutney, cut into small pieces
before combining with cream cheese.

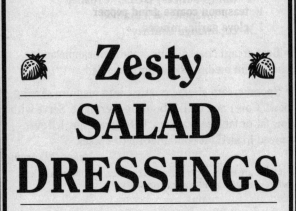

Zesty
SALAD
DRESSINGS

Buttermilk Pepper Dressing

1   cup buttermilk
½   cup MIRACLE WHIP® Salad Dressing
2   tablespoons KRAFT® 100% Grated
       Parmesan Cheese
1   teaspoon coarse grind pepper
1   clove garlic, minced

MIX all ingredients until well blended; refrigerate.
Serve with mixed salad greens.

Makes 1 cup dressing

Mock Blue Cheese Dressing

¾   cup buttermilk
¼   cup low-fat cottage cheese
2   tablespoons blue cheese, crumbled
2   teaspoons sugar
1   teaspoon lemon juice
¼   teaspoon celery seed
⅛   teaspoon black pepper
⅛   teaspoon salt
4   drops hot pepper sauce

In blender or food processor, blend all ingredients.
Chill, then serve over green salad.

Makes ¾ cup dressing

Favorite recipe from **The Sugar Association, Inc.**

Thousand Island Dressing

12 ounces (2 cartons) ALPINE LACE®
   Fat Free Cream Cheese with Garden
   Vegetables
½ cup 2% low-fat milk
⅓ cup fat-free sour cream
¼ cup chili sauce
¼ cup minced dill pickles
2 to 3 tablespoons minced red onion
2 tablespoons fresh lemon juice
¼ teaspoon hot red pepper sauce

1. In a medium-size bowl, whisk all of the ingredients together until well blended. Refrigerate until ready to serve.

2. Serve dressing over fish, meat or green salads.

Makes 2¼ cups dressing

Creamy Warm Bacon Dressing

4 slices OSCAR MAYER® Bacon, chopped
1 clove garlic, minced
1 cup MIRACLE WHIP® Salad Dressing
½ cup milk

COOK bacon until crisp. Drain, reserving 1 tablespoon drippings.

HEAT reserved drippings, chopped bacon and garlic over low heat 1 minute.

STIR in salad dressing and milk. Continue cooking, stirring occasionally, until thoroughly heated. Serve with spinach salad.   *Makes 1½ cups dressing*

Creamy Garlic Dressing

12 ounces (2 cartons) **ALPINE LACE®**
    Fat Free Cream Cheese with Garlic
    & Herbs
½ cup 2% low-fat milk
¼ cup fat-free sour cream
2 tablespoons fresh lemon juice
1 tablespoon prepared horseradish
½ teaspoon freshly ground black pepper
    Radish slices (optional)

1. In a food processor or blender, process all of the ingredients except radish slices for 30 seconds or until well blended. Refrigerate until ready to serve. Garnish with the radish slices, if you wish.

2. Serve dressing over vegetable or meat salads. It's also a great sauce for grilled meat, chicken and fish.

Makes 2 cups dressing

Yogurt Dressing

2 cups plain lowfat yogurt
4 teaspoons chopped fresh mint or
 ¼ teaspoon dried dill weed
⅛ teaspoon TABASCO® pepper sauce

In small bowl combine yogurt, mint and TABASCO®
sauce; mix well. Cover; refrigerate.

Makes 2 cups dressing

Chunky Cucumber Dill Dressing

1 cup peeled, chopped cucumber, divided
¾ cup plus 2 tablespoons plain nonfat
 yogurt
3 tablespoons fresh dill, chopped
2 teaspoons sugar
2 teaspoons lemon juice
⅛ teaspoon black pepper

In blender or food processor, blend ½ cup cucumber
with remaining ingredients. Stir in remaining ½ cup
cucumber. Chill, then serve over green salad or
chicken salad. *Makes about 6 servings*

Favorite recipe from **The Sugar Association, Inc.**

Fiesta Dressing

1 cup (8 ounces) plain yogurt
3 tablespoons minced onion
1½ tablespoons fresh lime juice
1 clove garlic, minced
1 teaspoon ground cumin
1 teaspoon chili powder
¼ teaspoon salt

Combine all ingredients in small bowl; mix well. Serve with cooked pasta or cabbage greens.

Makes 1 cup dressing

French Salad Dressing

½ teaspoon salt
1 clove garlic, crushed
¼ teaspoon dry mustard
¼ teaspoon freshly ground black pepper
¼ teaspoon dried salad seasoning
¼ cup white wine vinegar or lemon juice, divided
¼ cup FILIPPO BERIO® Olive Oil

In small bowl, combine salt, garlic, mustard, pepper and salad seasoning. Whisk in vinegar and olive oil until thoroughly mixed. Store dressing, in tightly covered container, in refrigerator up to 1 week. Shake well before using. *Makes about ½ cup dressing*

Lime and Lemon Cream Dressing

Finely grated peel and juice of 1 lime
Finely grated peel and juice of 1 lemon
2 teaspoons sugar
3 tablespoons FILIPPO BERIO®
Olive Oil
½ cup half-and-half
Few drops hot pepper sauce
2 shallots, finely chopped
Salt and freshly ground black pepper

In small bowl, combine lime peel and juice, lemon peel and juice and sugar. Whisk in olive oil. Gradually whisk in half-and-half and hot pepper sauce. Stir in shallots. Season to taste with salt and pepper. Store dressing, in tightly covered container, in refrigerator 1 to 2 days.

Makes about ¾ cup dressing

Basic Lemon Cream Dressing

2　cups nonfat cottage cheese
⅓　cup skim milk
¼　cup fresh lemon juice
2　teaspoons CRISCO® Vegetable Oil

Place cottage cheese, milk, lemon juice and Crisco® Oil in blender container. Blend at medium speed until smooth.   *Makes 2½ cups dressing*

Alternate Method: Mash cottage cheese with fork or potato masher. Place in container with tight-fitting lid. Add milk, lemon juice and Crisco® Oil. Shake well.

Tarragon and Celery Seed Dressing

¼ small yellow onion
3 tablespoons tarragon vinegar or white
    wine vinegar
2 tablespoons sugar
½ teaspoon salt
½ teaspoon dry mustard
¼ cup extra virgin olive oil
¼ cup vegetable oil
1 teaspoon celery seeds

Place onion and vinegar in food processor or blender; process until onion is finely chopped. Add sugar, salt and mustard. Process until blended.

With motor running, slowly pour olive and vegetable oils through feed tube. Process until smooth. Add celery seeds. Process until mixture is blended. Serve with mixed green, seafood or chicken salads.

Makes about 1 cup dressing

Lime Vinaigrette

3 tablespoons finely chopped fresh
    cilantro or parsley
3 tablespoons plain low-fat yogurt
3 tablespoons orange juice
2 tablespoons lime juice
2 tablespoons white wine vinegar
2 tablespoons water
1 tablespoon sugar
1 teaspoon chili powder
½ teaspoon onion powder
½ teaspoon ground cumin

In small jar with tight-fitting lid, combine all
ingredients. Shake well. Refrigerate until ready to use.
Shake before serving. Serve with seafood or chicken
salads. *Makes about ¾ cup dressing*

Classic Vinaigrette

¼ cup FILIPPO BERIO® Olive Oil
¼ cup white wine vinegar
1 teaspoon Dijon mustard
1 teaspoon sugar
  Salt and freshly ground black pepper

In small screw-topped jar, combine olive oil, vinegar,
mustard and sugar. Cover and shake vigorously until
well blended. Season to taste with salt and pepper.
Store dressing in refrigerator up to 1 week. Shake well
before using. *Makes about ½ cup dressing*

Garlic Vinaigrette: Add 1 small, halved garlic clove to
oil mixture; let stand 1 hour. Discard garlic. Store and
serve as directed above.

Lemon Vinaigrette: Use 2 tablespoons lemon juice in
place of vinegar; add finely grated peel of 1 small lemon
to oil mixture. Store and serve as directed above.

Herb Vinaigrette: Whisk 1 to 2 tablespoons finely
chopped fresh herbs (basil, oregano or chives) into
dressing just before serving. Store and serve as directed
above.

Shallot Vinaigrette: Add 1 to 2 finely chopped shallots
to oil mixture; let stand at least 1 hour before serving.
Store and serve as directed above.

Herb and Mustard Dressing

> 3   tablespoons balsamic or cider vinegar
> 1½   tablespoons Dijon mustard
> 1   tablespoon olive oil
> 1   teaspoon dried basil leaves
> 1   teaspoon dried thyme leaves
> 1   teaspoon dried rosemary
> 1   small clove garlic, minced

In small jar with tight-fitting lid, combine ¼ cup water, vinegar, mustard, oil, basil, thyme, rosemary and garlic. Shake well. Refrigerate until ready to use. Shake before serving. Serve with seafood or chicken salads.

Makes about ⅔ cup dressing

Sweet Mustard Dressing

¼ cup FILIPPO BERIO® Olive Oil
2 tablespoons honey
2 tablespoons white wine vinegar
4½ teaspoons Dijon-style mustard
1 tablespoon balsamic vinegar
   Salt and freshly ground black pepper

In small screw-topped jar, combine olive oil, honey, white wine vinegar, mustard and balsamic vinegar. Shake vigorously until well blended. Season to taste with salt and pepper. Store dressing in refrigerator up to 1 week. Shake well before using.

Makes about ½ cup dressing

Finger

FOODS

Fiesta Quesadillas with Fruit Salsa

1 can (11 ounces) DOLE® Mandarin
   Oranges, drained and finely chopped
1 tablespoon chopped fresh cilantro or
   parsley
1 tablespoon lime juice
4 (8-inch) whole wheat or flour tortillas
¾ cup (3 ounces) shredded low fat
   Monterey Jack, mozzarella or
   Cheddar cheese
⅔ cup finely chopped DOLE® Pitted Dates
   or Pitted Prunes
⅓ cup crumbled feta cheese
2 tablespoons chopped DOLE® Green
   Onion

• **Combine** mandarin oranges, cilantro and lime juice
in small bowl for salsa; set aside.

• **Place** 2 tortillas on large baking sheet. Sprinkle
shredded cheese, dates, feta cheese and green onion
over each tortilla to within ½ inch of edge; top with
remaining tortillas.

• **Bake** at 375°F 5 to 8 minutes or until hot. Cut each
quesadilla into 6 wedges.

• **Drain** salsa just before serving, if desired; serve over
warm quesadillas. Garnish with fresh cilantro sprigs, if
desired. *Makes 6 servings*

Easy Bean Nachos

24   (about 1 ounce) GUILTLESS
        GOURMET® Baked Tortilla Chips
        (yellow, white or blue corn)
½   cup GUILTLESS GOURMET® Bean Dip
        (Black or Pinto, mild or hot)
¼   cup chopped green onions
¼   cup GUILTLESS GOURMET® Nacho
        Dip (mild or spicy)
        Chopped red bell pepper strips
        (optional)

Microwave Directions: Spread tortilla chips on flat
microwave-safe plate. Dab 1 teaspoon bean dip on each
chip; sprinkle with onions. Dab ½ teaspoon nacho dip
on each chip. Microwave on HIGH (100% power)
30 seconds or until nacho dip starts to melt. Serve hot.
Garnish with red pepper, if desired.

Makes 24 nachos

Hint: To keep chips crisp and prevent them from
getting soggy, microwave each chip separately.

Conventional Directions: Preheat oven to 325°F.
Spread tortilla chips on baking sheet. Prepare nachos
as directed. Bake about 5 minutes or until nacho dip
starts to melt. Serve hot.

Philly® Free® Black Bean Spirals

4   ounces PHILADELPHIA BRAND®
      FREE® Fat Free Cream Cheese,
      softened
¼   cup BREAKSTONE'S® FREE® or
      KNUDSEN® FREE® Fat Free Sour
      Cream
¼   cup salsa
1   cup canned black beans, rinsed, drained
3   flour tortillas (6 inch)

BEAT cream cheese with electric mixer on medium speed until smooth. Add sour cream and salsa, mixing until blended.

PLACE beans in blender or food processor fitted with steel blade; cover. Blend until smooth. Spread thin layer of beans on each tortilla; spread cream cheese mixture over beans.

ROLL tortillas up tightly; cover. Refrigerate 30 minutes. Cut into ½-inch slices. Serve with salsa, if desired.   *Makes 12 servings*

Black Bean Tortilla Pinwheels

1 (8-ounce) package cream cheese, softened
1 cup sour cream
1 cup (4 ounces) shredded Wisconsin Monterey Jack cheese
¼ cup chopped red onion
¼ cup chopped drained pimiento-stuffed green olives
½ teaspoon seasoned salt
⅛ teaspoon garlic powder
1 (15-ounce) can black beans, drained
5 (10-inch) flour tortillas
   Salsa

Blend cream cheese and sour cream in medium bowl. Stir in Monterey Jack cheese, onion, olives, salt and garlic powder. Cover; refrigerate 2 hours. Process beans in food processor until smooth. Spread thin layer beans and thin layer cheese mixture over tortillas. Roll tortillas up tightly. Wrap in plastic wrap; refrigerate until chilled. Cut tortillas crosswise into ¾-inch-thick slices. Serve with salsa.

Makes 12 to 16 servings

Favorite recipe from **Wisconsin Milk Marketing Board**

Spam™ Pinwheels

1 (1-pound) loaf frozen bread dough,
   thawed
¼ cup pizza sauce
1 (7-ounce) can SPAM® Luncheon Meat,
   cubed
2 cups (8 ounces) shredded mozzarella
   cheese
2 tablespoons chopped pepperoncini
   Additional pizza sauce

Roll bread dough out onto lightly floured surface to
12-inch square. Brush pizza sauce over bread dough.
Sprinkle SPAM®, cheese and pepperoncini over dough.
Roll dough, jelly-roll fashion; pinch seam to seal (do
not seal ends). Cut roll into 16 slices. Place slices, cut-
side-down, on greased baking sheet. Cover and let rise
in warm place 45 minutes. Heat oven to 350°F. Bake
20 to 25 minutes or until golden brown. Serve
immediately with additional pizza sauce.

Makes 16 appetizer servings

Cucumber Canapés

1 cup cooked rice, cooled to room
  temperature
1 large tomato, peeled and diced
½ cup chopped fresh parsley
⅓ cup sliced green onions
¼ cup chopped mint leaves
2 cloves garlic, minced
3 tablespoons plain nonfat yogurt*
1 tablespoon lemon juice
1 tablespoon olive oil
¼ teaspoon ground white pepper
2 to 3 large cucumbers, peeled

Combine rice, tomato, parsley, onions, mint, garlic,
yogurt, lemon juice, oil, and pepper in large bowl.
Cover and refrigerate. Cut each cucumber crosswise
into ½-inch slices; hollow out center of each slice,
leaving bottom intact. Fill each cucumber slice with
scant tablespoon rice mixture.

Makes about 3 dozen canapés

*Substitute low-fat sour cream for yogurt, if desired.

Tip: Use ½ teaspoon measuring spoon to scoop seeds
from cucumbers.

Favorite recipe from **USA Rice Council**

Easy Vegetable Squares

2   cans (8 ounces each) refrigerated
    crescent rolls
1   package (8 ounces) cream cheese,
    softened
1   package (3 ounces) cream cheese,
    softened
⅓   cup mayonnaise
1   teaspoon dried dill weed, crushed
1   teaspoon buttermilk salad dressing mix
3   cups toppings*
1   cup (4 ounces) shredded Wisconsin
    Cheddar, Mozzarella or Monterey Jack
    cheese

Unroll crescent rolls and pat into 15½×10½×1-inch
baking pan. Bake according to package directions. Cool
on wire rack.

Meanwhile, blend cream cheese, mayonnaise, dill weed
and salad dressing mix in small bowl. Spread evenly
over crust. Sprinkle with desired toppings, then
shredded cheese. To serve, cut into squares.

Makes 32 appetizers

*Suggested Toppings: Finely chopped broccoli, cauliflower or green
bell pepper; seeded, chopped tomato; thinly sliced green onion, ripe
olives or celery; shredded carrot.

Favorite recipe from **Wisconsin Milk Marketing Board**

French-Style Pizza Bites

2 tablespoons olive oil
1 medium onion, thinly sliced
1 medium red bell pepper, cut into
     3-inch-long strips
2 cloves garlic, minced
⅓ cup pitted ripe olives, cut into thin
     wedges
1 can (10 ounces) refrigerated pizza crust
     dough
¾ cup (3 ounces) finely shredded Swiss
     or Gruyère cheese

Move oven rack to lowest position. Preheat oven to
425°F. Grease large baking sheet; set aside. Heat oil
until hot in medium skillet over medium heat. Add
onion, bell pepper and garlic. Cook and stir 5 minutes
until vegetables are crisp-tender. Stir in olives. Remove
from heat; set aside. Remove dough from can and pat
into 16×12-inch rectangle on prepared baking sheet.
Arrange vegetables over dough. Sprinkle with cheese.
Bake 10 minutes. With long spatula, loosen crust from
baking sheet. Slide pizza onto oven rack. Bake 3 to
5 minutes more until golden brown.

Slide baking sheet under pizza; remove from rack.
Transfer to cutting board. Cut pizza crosswise into
eight 1¾-inch-wide strips, then diagonally into ten
2-inch-wide strips, making diamond pieces. Serve
immediately.   *Makes about 24 servings*

Greek Grilled Pizza Wedges

⅓ cup prepared pizza sauce
¼ cup A.1.® Steak Sauce
4 (6-inch) whole wheat pita breads
2 tablespoons olive oil
4 ounces deli sliced roast beef, coarsely
  chopped
½ cup chopped tomato
⅓ cup sliced pitted ripe olives
½ cup (2 ounces) crumbled feta cheese*

In small bowl, combine pizza sauce and steak sauce; set aside. Brush both sides of pita breads with oil. Spread sauce mixture on one side of each pita; top with roast beef, tomato, olives and feta cheese.

Grill prepared pita, topping-side-up, over medium heat for 4 to 5 minutes or until toppings are hot and pita is crisp. Cut each pita into 4 wedges to serve.

Makes 8 appetizer servings

*¾ cup shredded mozzarella cheese may be substituted.

Mexican Pizzas

Red & Green Salsa (recipe follows)
(optional)
8 ounces chorizo sausage
1 cup (4 ounces) shredded mild Cheddar
cheese
1 cup (4 ounces) shredded Monterey Jack
cheese
3 (10-inch) flour tortillas

Prepare Red & Green Salsa; set aside. Remove and discard casing from chorizo. Heat medium skillet over high heat until hot. Reduce heat to medium. Crumble chorizo into skillet. Cook, stirring to separate meat, until no longer pink. Remove with slotted spoon; drain on paper towels.

Preheat oven to 450°F. Combine cheeses in small bowl. Place tortillas on baking sheets. Divide chorizo evenly among tortillas, leaving ½ inch of edges uncovered. Sprinkle cheese mixture over top.

Bake 8 to 10 minutes until edges are crisp and golden and cheese is bubbly and melted. Transfer to serving plates; cut each tortilla into 6 wedges. Sprinkle Red & Green Salsa on wedges, if desired.

Makes 6 to 8 appetizer servings

Red & Green Salsa

1 small red bell pepper
¼ cup coarsely chopped cilantro
3 green onions, cut into thin slices
2 fresh jalapeño chilies, seeded and
    minced*
2 tablespoons fresh lime juice
1 clove garlic, minced
¼ teaspoon salt

Cut bell pepper lengthwise in half; remove and discard
seeds and vein. Cut halves lengthwise into thin slivers;
cut slivers crosswise into halves. Mix all ingredients in
small bowl. Let stand, covered, at room temperature
1 to 2 hours to blend flavors.   *Makes 1 cup*

*When working with jalapeño chilies, wear plastic disposable gloves
and use caution to prevent irritation of skin and eyes.

Savory Bruschetta

¼ cup olive oil
1 clove garlic, minced
1 loaf (1 pound) French bread, cut in half
     lengthwise
1 package (8 ounces) PHILADELPHIA
     BRAND® Cream Cheese, softened
3 tablespoons KRAFT® 100% Grated
     Parmesan Cheese
2 tablespoons chopped pitted niçoise
     olives
1 cup chopped plum tomatoes
     Fresh basil leaves

MIX oil and garlic; spread on cut surfaces of bread. Bake at 400°F for 8 to 10 minutes or until toasted. Cool.

MIX cream cheese and Parmesan cheese with electric mixer on medium speed until blended. Stir in olives. Spread on cooled bread halves.

TOP with tomatoes and basil leaves. Cut diagonally into slices.   *Makes 2 dozen*

Pizza Bruschetta

1 loaf Italian bread, cut into ¼-inch-thick
    slices
1 cup prepared GOOD SEASONS® Italian
    or Zesty Italian Salad Dressing,
    divided
1 cup (4 ounces) KRAFT® Natural
    Shredded Low-Moisture Part-Skim
    Mozzarella Cheese
1 package (3 ounces) OSCAR MAYER®
    Authentic Pepperoni Slices, halved
1 large tomato, chopped
1 medium green bell pepper, chopped
¼ cup chopped green onions
6 pitted ripe olives, sliced
2 mushrooms, sliced

ARRANGE bread slices in single layer on baking
sheets. Brush with ½ cup of dressing.

BAKE at 450°F for 5 minutes or until golden brown.

MIX cheese, pepperoni, tomato, bell pepper, onions,
olives and mushrooms in medium bowl. Add
remaining ½ cup dressing; toss well. Spoon onto
toasted bread slices. Serve immediately.

Makes about 2 dozen

Pizzettes with Basil

⅔ cup (half of 15-ounce can)
CONTADINA® Dalla Casa Buitoni
Pizza Sauce with Italian Cheeses
1 package (3 ounces) cream cheese,
softened
2 tablespoons chopped fresh basil *or*
2 teaspoons dried basil, crushed
1 loaf (1 pound) Italian bread, cut into
¼-inch-thick slices, toasted
8 ounces (about 30) thin mozzarella
cheese slices
Fresh basil leaves (optional)
Freshly ground black pepper (optional)

COMBINE pizza sauce, cream cheese and chopped basil in small bowl. Mix well.

SPREAD 2 teaspoons pizza sauce mixture onto each toasted bread slice; top with 1 slice mozzarella cheese.

BROIL 3 to 4 inches from heat source for 1 to 2 minutes or until cheese is melted. Top with basil leaves and pepper, if desired.   *Makes 30 pizzettes*

Herb Crostini

32 slices (¼ inch thick) French bread
      (1 loaf)
      Olive oil
 1   container (15 ounces) POLLY-O® All
      Natural Whole Milk Ricotta Cheese
 1   envelope GOOD SEASONS® Italian
      Salad Dressing Mix
32 fresh basil leaves
 ½ cup roasted red pepper strips

ARRANGE bread slices in single layer on baking
sheets. Brush with oil.

BAKE at 450°F for 5 to 8 minutes or until golden
brown. Cool.

MIX cheese and salad dressing mix in small bowl until
well blended. Spread about 1 tablespoon cheese
mixture on each toasted bread slice. Top with basil leaf
and pepper strip. Serve immediately.

Makes 32 crostini

Italian Tomato Bread

3½ cups (two 14-ounce cans)
        CONTADINA® Dalla Casa Buitoni
        Pasta Ready Chunky Tomatoes with
        Three Cheeses, undrained
 ¼ cup sliced green onions
 1 loaf (1 pound) Italian or French bread
1½ cups (6 ounces) shredded mozzarella
        cheese

COMBINE tomatoes and green onions in medium
bowl. Cut bread in half lengthwise; scoop out
½-inch-deep layer of bread to within 1 inch of crust.
Spoon tomato mixture into crust; top with cheese.
Place on baking sheet.

BAKE in preheated 450°F oven for 5 to 8 minutes or
until heated through and cheese is melted. Cut into
1-inch slices.   *Makes about 24 appetizers*

Holiday Appetizer Puffs

1 **sheet frozen puff pastry, thawed (½ of 17¼-ounce package)**
2 **tablespoons olive or vegetable oil**
  Toppings: grated Parmesan cheese, sesame seeds, poppy seeds, dried dill weed, dried basil, paprika, drained capers, green olive slices

Preheat oven to 425°F. Roll out pastry on lightly floured surface to 13×13-inch square. Cut into shapes with cookie cutters (simple shaped cutters work best). Place on ungreased baking sheets.

Brush cutouts lightly with oil. Decorate with desired toppings.

Bake 6 to 8 minutes or until golden. Serve warm or at room temperature.

Makes about 1½ dozen appetizers

Venetian Canapés

12 slices firm white bread
 5 tablespoons butter or margarine,
    divided
 2 tablespoons all-purpose flour
 ½ cup milk
 3 ounces fresh mushrooms
    (about 9 medium), finely chopped
 6 tablespoons grated Parmesan cheese,
    divided
 2 teaspoons anchovy paste
 ¼ teaspoon salt
 ⅛ teaspoon ground black pepper
    Green and ripe olive slices, red and
       green bell pepper strips and rolled
       anchovy fillets, for garnish

Preheat oven to 350°F. Cut rounds out of bread slices
with 2-inch round cutter. Melt 3 tablespoons butter in
small saucepan. Brush both sides of bread rounds
lightly with melted butter. Bake bread rounds on
ungreased baking sheets 5 to 6 minutes per side or
until golden. Remove to wire rack. Cool completely.
Increase oven temperature to 425°F.

Melt remaining 2 tablespoons butter in same small saucepan. Stir in flour; cook and stir over medium heat until bubbly. Whisk in milk; cook and stir 1 minute or until sauce thickens and bubbles. (Sauce will be very thick.) Place mushrooms in large bowl; stir in sauce, 3 tablespoons cheese, anchovy paste, salt and black pepper until well blended.

Spread heaping teaspoonful mushroom mixture onto each toast round; place on ungreased baking sheets. Sprinkle remaining 3 tablespoons cheese over bread rounds, dividing evenly. Garnish, if desired. Bake 5 to 7 minutes or until tops are light brown. Serve warm.

Makes 8 to 10 servings

Potato Skins with Cheddar Melt

 4 medium-size Idaho baking potatoes
    (about 2 pounds)
 4 slices lean turkey bacon
 2 tablespoons vegetable oil
 2 cups (8 ounces) shredded ALPINE
    LACE® Reduced Fat Cheddar Cheese
 ¼ cup fat free sour cream
 2 tablespoons finely chopped chives or
    green onions
 1 tablespoon minced jalapeño pepper

1. Place a piece of foil on the bottom rack of the oven and preheat the oven to 425°F. Scrub the potatoes well and pierce the skins a few times with a sharp knife. Place the potatoes directly on the middle oven rack and bake for 1 hour or until soft.

2. Meanwhile, in a small skillet, cook the bacon over medium heat until crisp. Drain on paper towels, then crumble the bacon.

3. Using a serrated knife, cut the potatoes in half lengthwise. With a small spoon, scoop out the pulp, leaving a ¼-inch-thick shell. (Save the potato pulp for another use.) Cut the skins into appetizer-size triangles.

4. Place the skins on a baking sheet, brush the insides with the oil and bake for 15 minutes or until crisp.

5. Remove the skins from the oven, sprinkle with the cheese and return to the oven for 5 minutes or until the cheese melts. Top the skins with the sour cream, then sprinkle with the chives, jalapeño pepper and bacon.   *Makes about 24 appetizers*

Spring Rolls

1   cup shredded cabbage or coleslaw mix
½   cup finely chopped cooked ham
¼   cup finely chopped water chestnuts
¼   cup sliced green onions
3   tablespoons plum sauce, divided
1   teaspoon Oriental sesame oil
3   flour tortillas (6 to 7 inches)

1. Combine cabbage, ham, water chestnuts, green onions, 2 tablespoons plum sauce and oil in medium bowl; mix well.

2. Spread remaining 1 tablespoon plum sauce evenly over tortillas. Spread about ½ cup cabbage mixture on each tortilla to within ¼ inch of edge; roll up.

3. Wrap each tortilla tightly in plastic wrap. Refrigerate at least 1 hour or up to 24 hours before serving.

4. Cut each tortilla into 4 pieces.

Makes 12 servings

Baked Garlic Bundles

½ of 16-ounce package frozen phyllo
   dough, thawed to room temperature
¾ cup butter, melted
3 large heads fresh California garlic,*
   separated into cloves, peeled
½ cup finely chopped walnuts
1 cup Italian-style bread crumbs

Preheat oven to 350°F. Remove phyllo from package;
unroll and place on large sheet of waxed paper. Using
scissors, cut phyllo crosswise into 2-inch-wide strips.
Cover with large sheet of waxed paper and damp
kitchen towel. (Phyllo dries out quickly if not covered.)

Lay 1 phyllo strip on flat surface; brush immediately
with melted butter. Place 1 clove of garlic at 1 end of
strip. Sprinkle about 1 teaspoon walnuts over length of
strip. Roll up garlic clove and walnuts in phyllo strip,
tucking in side edges as you roll. Brush bundle with
melted butter; roll in bread crumbs to coat. Repeat
with remaining phyllo strips, garlic cloves, walnuts,
butter and bread crumbs until all but smallest garlic
cloves are used. Place bundles on rack in shallow
roasting pan. Bake 20 minutes or until crispy.

Makes 24 to 27 appetizers

*The whole garlic bulb is called a head.

Favorite recipe from **Christopher Ranch Garlic**

Angelic Deviled Eggs

6 **large eggs**
¼ **cup 1% low-fat cottage cheese**
3 **tablespoons fat-free ranch dressing**
2 **teaspoons Dijon mustard**
2 **tablespoons minced fresh chives or dill**
1 **tablespoon diced well-drained pimiento
 or roasted red pepper**

1. Place eggs in medium saucepan; add enough water to cover. Bring to a boil over medium heat, stirring gently and frequently. Remove from heat; cover. Let stand 20 minutes. Drain. Add cold water to eggs in saucepan; let stand until eggs are cool. Drain. Tap eggs gently on work surface to crack shells. Remove shells; discard.

2. Cut eggs lengthwise in half. Remove yolks, reserving 3 yolk halves. Discard remaining yolks or reserve for another use. Place egg whites, cut sides up, on serving plate; cover with plastic wrap. Refrigerate while preparing filling.

3. Combine cottage cheese, ranch dressing, mustard and reserved yolk halves in mini food processor; process until smooth. (Or, place in small bowl and mash with fork until well blended.) Transfer cheese mixture to small bowl; stir in chives and pimiento. Spoon into egg whites; cover with plastic wrap. Refrigerate until chilled, at least 1 hour. Garnish, if desired. *Makes 12 servings*

Baked Mozzarella Sticks

Butter-flavored nonstick cooking spray
12 **ounces (2 blocks) ALPINE LACE® Fat
Free Pasteurized Process Skim Milk
Cheese Product—For Mozzarella
Lovers**
½ **cup egg substitute** *or* **2 large eggs**
1 **cup Italian-seasoned dry bread crumbs**
¼ **cup minced fresh parsley**

1. Preheat the oven to 400°F. Spray 2 large baking sheets with the cooking spray.

2. Cut each block of cheese in half crosswise, then each half lengthwise into 3 equal sticks (about 3×¾ inches), making a total of 12 sticks.

3. In a medium-size bowl, whisk the egg substitute (or the whole eggs) until frothy. On a plate, toss the bread crumbs with the parsley.

4. Dip each cheese stick first into the egg substitute, then roll in the bread crumbs, pressing them lightly as you go. Arrange the cheese in a single layer on the baking sheets.

5. Spray the sticks lightly with the cooking spray. Bake for 10 minutes or until golden brown and crispy.

Makes 12 cheese sticks

Spinach Cheese Triangles

1   package (8 ounces) PHILADELPHIA
      BRAND® Cream Cheese, softened
1   package (10 ounces) frozen chopped
      spinach, thawed, well drained
⅓   cup chopped drained roasted red
      peppers
¼   teaspoon garlic salt
6   sheets frozen phyllo, thawed
½   cup (1 stick) butter or margarine,
      melted

MIX cream cheese, spinach, red peppers and garlic salt
with electric mixer on medium speed until well
blended.

LAY 1 phyllo sheet on flat surface. Brush with some of
the melted butter. Cut lengthwise into 4 (18×3½-inch)
strips.

SPOON about 1 tablespoon filling about 1 inch from
one end of each strip. Fold the end over the filling at a
45-degree angle. Continue folding as you would fold a
flat to form a triangle that encloses filling. Repeat
procedure with remaining phyllo sheets. Place
triangles on cookie sheet. Brush with melted butter.

BAKE at 375°F for 12 to 15 minutes or until golden
brown.   *Makes 2 dozen*

Tip: Unfold phyllo sheets; cover with waxed paper and
damp towel to prevent drying until ready to use.

Savory Stuffed Mushrooms

24   **large mushrooms**
½   **cup chopped green onions**
1   **tablespoon margarine or butter**
½   **teaspoon dried rosemary leaves**
¼   **cup dry white wine**
¼   **cup GREY POUPON® COUNTRY
     DIJON® Mustard**
¾   **cup plain dry bread crumbs**
¾   **cup shredded Swiss cheese (3 ounces)**
1   **egg, beaten**
4   **slices bacon, cooked and crumbled
     Chopped parsley and grated Parmesan
     cheese, for garnish**

Remove stems from mushrooms; reserve caps.
Coarsely chop mushroom stems. In large skillet, over
medium-high heat, sauté chopped stems and green
onions in margarine or butter until tender. Stir in
rosemary, wine and mustard; heat to a boil. Reduce
heat to low; simmer for 3 minutes. Remove from heat;
let stand 5 minutes. Stir in bread crumbs, cheese, egg
and bacon. Spoon stuffing mixture into mushroom
caps; place on baking sheet. Bake at 350°F for 12 to
15 minutes or until heated through. Garnish with
parsley and cheese. Serve hot.

Makes 24 appetizers

Pesto-Stuffed Mushrooms

12   **medium mushroom caps, wiped clean**
⅔   **cup prepared basil pesto**
¼   **cup grated Parmesan cheese**
¼   **cup chopped roasted red pepper**
3   **tablespoons seasoned bread crumbs**
3   **tablespoons pine nuts**
¼   **cup (1 ounce) shredded mozzarella
    cheese**

1. Preheat oven to 400°F. Place mushroom caps, stem-side-up, on baking sheet.

2. Combine pesto, Parmesan cheese, red pepper, bread crumbs and pine nuts in small bowl; mix until well blended.

3. Fill mushroom caps with pesto mixture. Sprinkle each with mozzarella cheese. Bake 8 to 10 minutes or until filling is hot and cheese is melted. Serve immediately.   *Makes 12 mushrooms*

Grilled Stuffed Mushrooms

24 large (2 inches each) mushrooms,
    wiped clean
3 tablespoons olive oil, divided
1 red bell pepper, seeded and chopped
½ cup minced fresh Italian parsley
2 tablespoons FRENCH'S®
    Worcestershire Sauce
1 teaspoon garlic powder
1⅓ cups (2.8-ounce can) FRENCH'S®
    French Fried Onions, divided
½ cup grated Parmesan cheese

Remove stems from mushrooms. Finely chop stems;
set aside. Brush mushroom caps with *1 tablespoon* oil.
Place caps on a tray. Heat remaining *2 tablespoons* oil
in large skillet over medium-high heat. Add chopped
stems and pepper; cook and stir until tender. Stir in
parsley, Worcestershire and garlic powder. Cook until
liquid is evaporated, stirring often. Stir in ⅔ *cup*
French Fried Onions and cheese.

Spoon about 1 tablespoon mushroom mixture into
each mushroom cap. Place mushroom caps on
vegetable grilling rack or basket. Place on grid. Grill
over medium-high coals 15 minutes or until
mushrooms are tender. Sprinkle with remaining ⅔ *cup*
French Fried Onions. Grill 1 minute or until onions
are golden. Serve warm.

Makes 6 appetizer servings

Tri-Colored Tuna Stuffed Mushrooms

- 30 medium mushrooms, cleaned and
      stems removed
- 2 tablespoons melted butter or margarine
- 1 cup finely chopped onions
- 1 tablespoon vegetable oil
- 1 can (6 ounces) STARKIST® Solid
     White or Chunk Light Tuna, drained
     and flaked
- ½ cup shredded smoked Gouda cheese,
     divided
- 1 red bell pepper, seeded and puréed*
- 1 package (10 ounces) frozen spinach
     soufflé
- ¼ cup mayonnaise, divided
- ¼ cup grated Parmesan cheese, divided
- ½ teaspoon curry powder

Lightly coat mushroom caps with melted butter; divide
into 3 groups of 10. Sauté onions in hot oil until
tender. *In each of 3 small bowls,* place ⅓ tuna and
⅓ sautéed onions. In first small bowl, add ¼ cup Gouda
cheese and red bell pepper purée. In second small bowl,
add ¼ cup spinach souffle,** 2 tablespoons
mayonnaise, 2 tablespoons Parmesan cheese and curry
powder. In third small bowl, add remaining ¼ cup
Gouda cheese, remaining 2 tablespoons mayonnaise
and remaining 2 tablespoons Parmesan cheese.

Fill 10 mushrooms with filling from each bowl.
Arrange on baking sheet; bake in 350°F oven 10 to 12
minutes. Serve hot. *Makes 30 servings*

*To purée bell pepper: place seeded and coarsely chopped red pepper in blender or food processor with metal blade. Blend or process until puréed.

**Keep remainder frozen until ready to use.

Mini Tuna Tarts

1　can (6 ounces) STARKIST® Solid
　　White or Chunk Light Tuna, drained
　　and flaked
2　tablespoons mayonnaise
2　tablespoons sweet pickle relish
1　green onion, including top, minced
¾　cup shredded Monterey Jack cheese
　　Salt and pepper to taste
1　package (10 count) refrigerated flaky
　　biscuits

Combine tuna, mayonnaise, pickle relish, onion and cheese; mix well. Add salt and pepper. Separate each biscuit into halves. Press each half in bottom of lightly greased muffin pan to form a cup. Spoon scant tablespoon tuna mixture into each muffin cup. Bake in 400°F oven 8 to 10 minutes or until edges of biscuits are just golden. Serve hot or cold.

Makes 20 servings

Tuna in Crispy Won Ton Cups

18 won ton skins, *each* 3¼ inches square
    Butter or olive oil cooking spray
 1 can (6 ounces) STARKIST® Solid
    White or Chunk Light Tuna, drained
    and flaked
⅓ cup cold cooked orzo (rice-shaped
    pasta) or cooked rice
¼ cup southwestern ranch-style vegetable
    dip with jalapeños or other sour
    cream dip
¼ cup drained pimiento-stuffed green
    olives, chopped
 3 tablespoons sweet pickle relish, drained
    Paprika, for garnish
    Parsley sprigs, for garnish

Cut won tons into circles with 3-inch round cookie
cutter. Spray miniature muffin pans with cooking
spray. Place one circle in each muffin cup; press to
sides to mold won ton to cup. Spray each won ton with
cooking spray. Bake in 350°F oven 6 to 8 minutes or
until golden brown; set aside.

In small bowl, gently mix tuna, orzo, dip, olives and
relish. Refrigerate filling until ready to serve. Remove
won ton cups from muffin pan. Use rounded teaspoon
to fill each cup; garnish with paprika and parsley.

Makes 18 servings

Tuna 'n' Celery Sticks

- **4** ounces cream cheese, softened
- **3** tablespoons plain yogurt or mayonnaise
- **1½** teaspoons dried basil
- **1** can (12 ounces) STARKIST® Solid White or Chunk Light Tuna, drained and flaked
- **½** cup finely grated carrot or zucchini
- **½** cup finely shredded Cheddar cheese
- **2** teaspoons instant minced onion
- **10** to 12 celery stalks, cleaned, strings removed

In large bowl, mix together cream cheese, yogurt and basil until smooth. Add tuna, carrot, Cheddar cheese and onion; mix well. Spread mixture in celery stalks; cut into fourths. *Makes 40 servings*

Steamed and Spiced Shrimp

- **1** pound raw medium shrimp in the shell
- **2** teaspoons oil
- **1** tablespoon prepared seafood seasoning

Place shrimp in medium bowl. Cover shrimp with oil and seafood seasoning; toss to coat. Place shrimp on steamer rack over boiling water. Reduce heat and steam, covered, about 2 to 3 minutes or until bright pink and opaque. Serve with cocktail sauce, if desired.
Makes about 40 pieces

Favorite recipe from **National Fisheries Institute**

Seafood Cocktail Puffs

Spicy Party Dip (recipe follows)
1 package (1 ounce) HIDDEN VALLEY
   RANCH® Milk Recipe Original
   Ranch® salad dressing mix
1½ cups biscuit mix
8 ounces shrimp, chopped, or crabmeat,
   fresh or frozen and thawed
1 egg
⅓ cup milk
   Vegetable oil, for deep frying
   Lemon wedges and parsley sprigs

Prepare Spicy Party Dip. In medium bowl, combine salad dressing mix with biscuit mix. Toss with shrimp. In separate bowl, whisk together egg and milk. Add to shrimp mixture, combining well. In deep fryer or deep saucepan, heat ½ inch oil to 375°F. Drop rounded teaspoons of batter into oil, one at a time. Fry in batches until brown, 2 to 3 minutes, turning to brown. Remove with slotted spoon; drain on paper towels. Arrange on serving platter garnished with lemon wedges and parsley. Serve with Spicy Party Dip.

Makes 6 to 8 servings

Spicy Party Dip

1 cup prepared HIDDEN VALLEY
   RANCH® Original Ranch® salad
   dressing
2 tablespoons lemon juice
1 tablespoon Dijon mustard
¼ teaspoon hot pepper sauce
   Dash of Worcestershire sauce

In medium bowl, whisk together all ingredients. Refrigerate until ready to serve with Seafood Cocktail Puffs.

Makes about 1 cup dip

Chilled Shrimp in Chinese Mustard Sauce

- 1 cup water
- ½ cup dry white wine
- 2 tablespoons low-sodium soy sauce
- ½ teaspoon Szechuan or black peppercorns
- 1 pound raw large shrimp, peeled, deveined
- ¼ cup prepared sweet and sour sauce
- 2 teaspoons hot Chinese mustard

1. Combine water, wine, soy sauce and peppercorns in medium saucepan. Bring to a boil over high heat. Add shrimp; reduce heat to medium. Cover and simmer 2 to 3 minutes until shrimp are pink and opaque. Drain well. Cover and refrigerate until chilled.

2. Combine sweet and sour sauce and mustard in small bowl; mix well. Serve as dipping sauce for shrimp.

Makes 6 servings

Empandillas

½ pound ground beef
1 cup chopped ripe olives
¾ cup chopped fresh mushrooms
¼ cup water
1 package (1.0 ounces) LAWRY'S® Taco
    Spices & Seasonings
1 package (17¼ ounces) frozen puff
    pastry sheets, thawed
1 egg white, beaten

In medium bowl, combine ground beef, olives, mushrooms, water and Taco Spices & Seasonings; blend well. Roll each pastry sheet into 12-inch square. Cut each sheet into 9 squares. Place approximately 2 teaspoons meat mixture in center of each square; moisten edges with water. Fold one corner over to form triangle and pinch edges together to seal. Brush with egg white. Place on ungreased baking sheet. Bake in 375°F oven 15 to 20 minutes or until golden brown.

Makes 18 appetizers

Hints: Two cans (9 ounces each) refrigerated crescent roll dough can be used in place of puff pastry sheets. Roll out dough into two 12-inch squares. Follow directions above. Stir 3 tablespoons grated cheese into the filling for extra flavor.

Spicy Beef Saté

1   **cup chopped green onions**
½   **cup A.1.® THICK & HEARTY® Steak
      Sauce**
½   **cup chunky or creamy peanut butter**
¼   **cup lemon juice**
¼   **cup firmly packed light brown sugar**
¼   **cup vegetable oil**
¼   **teaspoon crushed red pepper flakes**
2   **cloves garlic, minced**
1   **(1-pound) beef flank steak, thinly sliced
      across grain**

Soak 24 (10-inch) wooden skewers in water at least 30
minutes.

In medium nonmetal bowl, combine green onions,
steak sauce, peanut butter, juice, sugar, oil, pepper
flakes and garlic; add steak strips, stirring to coat.
Cover; refrigerate 1 hour, stirring occasionally.

Remove steak from marinade; reserve marinade.
Thread steak strips onto skewers. Grill skewers over
medium heat or broil 6 inches from heat source
15 minutes or to desired doneness, turning and basting
often with marinade. (Discard any remaining
marinade.) Serve immediately.

Makes 24 appetizers

East Meets West Cocktail Franks

1   cup prepared sweet and sour sauce
1½ tablespoons rice vinegar or cider
      vinegar
1   tablespoon grated fresh ginger *or*
      1 teaspoon dried ginger
1   tablespoon Oriental sesame oil
½   teaspoon chile oil (optional)
1   package (12 ounces) HEBREW
      NATIONAL® Cocktail Beef Franks
2   tablespoons chopped cilantro or chives

Combine sweet and sour sauce, vinegar, ginger, sesame oil and chile oil in medium saucepan. Bring to a boil over medium heat. Cook 5 minutes or until thickened. Add cocktail franks; cover and cook until heated through. Transfer to chafing dish; sprinkle with cilantro. Serve with frilled wooden picks.

Makes 12 appetizer servings
(2 cocktail franks per serving)

Beefy Tortilla Rolls

¼ cup GREY POUPON® COUNTRY
    DIJON® Mustard
3 ounces cream cheese, softened
2 teaspoons prepared horseradish
2 teaspoons chopped cilantro or parsley
2 (10-inch) flour tortillas
1 cup torn spinach leaves
6 ounces thinly sliced deli roast beef
1 large tomato, cut into 8 slices
    Lettuce leaves

In small bowl, combine mustard, cream cheese,
horseradish and cilantro. Spread each flour tortilla
with half the mustard mixture. Top each with half the
spinach leaves, roast beef and tomato slices. Roll up
each tortilla jelly-roll fashion. Wrap each roll in plastic
wrap and chill at least 1 hour.*

To serve, cut each roll into 10 slices; arrange on
lettuce-lined platter.   *Makes 20 appetizers*

*Tortilla rolls may be frozen. To serve, thaw at room temperature for
1 hour before slicing.

Honey Dijon Barbecue Ribettes

2½ **pounds baby back pork spareribs, split**
 2 **cloves garlic, minced**
 1 **tablespoon vegetable oil**
⅔ **cup chili sauce**
⅓ **cup GREY POUPON® Dijon Mustard**
¼ **cup honey**
 6 **thin lemon slices**
½ **teaspoon liquid hot pepper seasoning**

Place ribs in large heavy pot; fill pot with water to cover ribs. Over high heat, heat to a boil; reduce heat. Cover; simmer for 30 to 40 minutes or until ribs are tender. Drain.

Meanwhile, in medium saucepan, over low heat, cook garlic in oil until tender. Stir in chili sauce, mustard, honey, lemon slices and hot pepper seasoning. Cook over medium heat until heated through, about 2 to 3 minutes. Brush ribs with prepared sauce. Grill over medium heat for 15 to 20 minutes or until done, turning and brushing often with remaining sauce. Slice into individual pieces to serve; garnish as desired. Serve hot.   *Makes 8 servings*

Corned Beef & Swiss Appetizers

1　package (8 ounces) PHILADELPHIA
　　　BRAND® Cream Cheese, softened
2　teaspoons Dijon mustard
¼　pound corned beef, chopped
½　cup (2 ounces) KRAFT® Natural
　　　Shredded Swiss Cheese
2　tablespoons chopped green onion
36　slices cocktail rye bread, toasted

MIX cream cheese and mustard with electric mixer on medium speed until smooth.

BLEND in corned beef, Swiss cheese and onion. Spread on toast slices. Place on baking sheet.

BROIL 2 to 3 minutes or until lightly browned.

Makes 3 dozen appetizers

Reuben Rolls

⅓ cup HELLMANN'S® or BEST FOODS®
   Real or Light Mayonnaise or Low Fat
   Mayonnaise Dressing
1 tablespoon Dijon mustard
½ teaspoon caraway seeds
1 cup (4 ounces) cooked corned beef,
   finely chopped
1 cup (4 ounces) shredded Swiss cheese
1 cup sauerkraut, rinsed, drained and
   patted dry with paper towels
1 package (10 ounces) refrigerated pizza
   crust dough

1. Preheat oven to 420°F. In medium bowl, combine mayonnaise, mustard and caraway seeds. Add corned beef, cheese and sauerkraut; toss to blend well.

2. Unroll dough onto large ungreased cookie sheet. Gently stretch to 14×12-inch rectangle. Cut dough lengthwise in half.

3. Spoon half of the filling onto each piece, spreading to within 1 inch from edges. Starting from long side, roll each jelly-roll style; pinch to seal edges. Arrange rolls, seam-side-down, 3 inches apart.

4. Bake 10 minutes or until golden brown. Let stand 5 minutes. Cut into 1-inch slices.

Makes about 30 appetizers

Mini Sausage Quiches

½ cup butter or margarine, softened
3 ounces cream cheese, softened
1 cup all-purpose flour
½ pound BOB EVANS FARMS® Italian
     Roll Sausage
1 cup (4 ounces) shredded Swiss cheese
1 tablespoon snipped fresh chives
2 eggs
1 cup half-and-half
¼ teaspoon salt
   Dash cayenne pepper

Beat butter and cream cheese in medium bowl until creamy. Blend in flour; refrigerate 1 hour. Roll into 24 (1-inch) balls; press each into ungreased mini-muffin cup to form pastry shell.

Preheat oven to 375°F. To prepare filling, crumble sausage into small skillet. Cook over medium heat until browned, stirring occasionally. Drain off any drippings. Sprinkle evenly into pastry shells in muffin cups; sprinkle with Swiss cheese and chives. Whisk eggs, half-and-half, salt and cayenne until blended; pour into pastry shells.

Bake 20 to 30 minutes or until set. Remove from pans. Serve hot. Refrigerate leftovers.

Makes 24 appetizers

Antipasto Platter

¼ cup GREY POUPON® Dijon Mustard
¼ cup sour cream*
¼ cup buttermilk
¼ cup grated Parmesan cheese
1 teaspoon coarsely ground black pepper
½ head leaf lettuce, separated into leaves
2 ounces radicchio leaves
1 bunch endive, separated into leaves
8 ounces deli sliced ham
4 ounces deli sliced Swiss cheese
2 ounces deli sliced salami
1 medium tomato, cut into wedges
¼ cup whole ripe olives

In small bowl, whisk mustard, sour cream, buttermilk, Parmesan cheese and pepper until blended. Chill dressing until serving time.

Place lettuce, radicchio and endive on large serving platter; top with ham, Swiss cheese, salami, tomato and olives. Serve with prepared dressing.

Makes 4 servings

*Low-fat sour cream may be substituted for regular sour cream.

Southwest Chicken Fingers

⅔ cup HELLMANN'S® or BEST FOODS®
    Real or Light Mayonnaise or Low Fat
    Mayonnaise Dressing
⅓ cup prepared salsa
1½ pounds boneless skinless chicken
    breasts, cut into 3 × 1-inch strips

1. In large bowl combine mayonnaise and salsa; reserve 6 tablespoons.

2. Add chicken strips to mayonnaise mixture in large bowl; toss well. Let stand 30 minutes.

3. Grill chicken 5 inches from heat, turning once, 4 minutes or until chicken is tender. Or, broil, without turning, 5 inches from heat.

4. Serve with reserved sauce.

Makes 6 to 8 appetizer servings

Indonesian Satay

¼ cup lime juice
2 cloves garlic, minced
1 teaspoon grated lime peel
½ teaspoon ground ginger
½ teaspoon ground red pepper
4 boneless skinless chicken breasts
(about 2 pounds), cut into strips
Spicy Peanut Sauce (recipe follows)

• Mix together lime juice, garlic, peel, ginger and pepper; pour over chicken. Cover. Refrigerate 1 hour. Drain. Prepare Spicy Peanut Sauce.

• Prepare coals for grilling.

• Thread chicken onto individual skewers; place on greased grill over hot coals (coals should be glowing).

• Grill, uncovered, 3 to 5 minutes on each side or until tender. Serve with Spicy Peanut Sauce.

Makes 15 servings

Spicy Peanut Sauce

1 package (8 ounces) PHILADELPHIA
BRAND® Cream Cheese, cubed
½ cup milk
3 tablespoons peanut butter
2 tablespoons brown sugar
½ teaspoon ground cardamom
⅛ teaspoon ground red pepper

• Stir ingredients in small saucepan over low heat until smooth.

Chicken Kabobs with Thai Dipping Sauce

1 **pound boneless skinless chicken breasts, cut into 1-inch cubes**
1 **small cucumber, seeded and cut into small chunks**
1 **cup cherry tomatoes**
2 **green onions, cut into 1-inch pieces**
⅔ **cup teriyaki baste & glaze sauce**
⅓ **cup FRANK'S® Original REDHOT® Cayenne Pepper Sauce**
⅛ **cup peanut butter**
3 **tablespoons frozen orange juice concentrate, undiluted**
2 **cloves garlic, minced**

Thread chicken, cucumber, tomatoes and onions alternately onto metal skewers; set aside.

To prepare Thai Dipping Sauce, combine teriyaki baste & glaze sauce, RedHot® sauce, peanut butter, orange juice concentrate and garlic; mix well. Reserve ⅔ *cup* sauce for dipping.

Brush skewers with some of remaining sauce. Place skewers on oiled grid. Grill over high heat 10 minutes or until chicken is no longer pink in centers, turning and basting often with remaining sauce. Serve skewers with reserved Thai Dipping Sauce. Garnish as desired.

Makes 6 appetizer servings

Buffalo Chicken Wings

24	chicken wings
1	teaspoon salt
¼	teaspoon ground black pepper
4	cups vegetable oil, for frying
¼	cup butter or margarine
¼	cup hot pepper sauce
1	teaspoon white wine vinegar
	Celery sticks
1	bottle (8 ounces) blue cheese dressing

Cut tips off wings at first joint; discard tips. Cut
remaining wings into two parts at the joint; sprinkle
with salt and pepper. Heat oil in deep fryer or heavy
saucepan to 375°F. Add half the wings; fry about 10
minutes or until golden brown and crisp, stirring
occasionally. Remove with slotted spoon; drain on
paper towels. Repeat with remaining wings. Melt butter
in small saucepan over medium heat; stir in pepper
sauce and vinegar. Cook until thoroughly heated. Place
wings on large platter. Pour sauce over wings. Serve
warm with celery and dressing for dipping.

Makes 24 appetizers

Favorite recipe from **National Broiler Council**

Almond Chicken Kabobs

⅓ cup A.1.® Steak Sauce
1 tablespoon Dijon mustard
1 tablespoon honey
1 tablespoon vegetable oil
1 tablespoon lemon juice
1 clove garlic, crushed
4 boneless chicken breast halves
     (about 1 pound)
¼ cup toasted slivered almonds, finely
     chopped

In small bowl, combine steak sauce, mustard, honey,
oil, lemon juice and garlic; set aside.

Cut each chicken breast half into 8 cubes. In medium
nonmetal bowl, combine chicken cubes and ½ cup steak
sauce mixture. Cover; chill 1 hour, turning
occasionally.

Soak 16 (10-inch) wooden skewers in hot water at least
30 minutes. Thread 2 chicken cubes onto each skewer.
Grill kabobs over medium heat 6 to 8 minutes or until
done, turning and brushing with remaining sauce.
Remove from grill; quickly roll kabobs in almonds.
Serve immediately.   *Makes 16 appetizers*

Garlicky Gilroy Chicken Wings

2 **pounds chicken wings (about 15 wings)**
3 **heads fresh California garlic,* separated into cloves and peeled**
1 **cup plus 1 tablespoon olive oil, divided**
10 **to 15 drops TABASCO® pepper sauce**
1 **cup grated Parmesan cheese**
1 **cup Italian-style dry bread crumbs**
1 **teaspoon black pepper**

Preheat oven to 375°F. Disjoint chicken wings, removing tips. (If desired, save tips to make chicken stock.) Rinse wings; pat dry. Place garlic, 1 cup oil and TABASCO® sauce in food processor or blender container; cover and process until smooth. Pour garlic mixture into small bowl. Combine cheese, bread crumbs and black pepper in shallow dish. Dip wings into garlic mixture, then roll, one at a time, in crumb mixture until thoroughly coated. Brush shallow nonstick pan with remaining 1 tablespoon oil; arrange wings in a single layer. Drizzle remaining garlic mixture over wings; sprinkle with remaining crumb mixture. Bake 45 to 60 minutes or until brown and crisp. Garnish as desired.

Makes about 6 appetizer servings

*The whole garlic bulb is called a head.

Favorite recipe from **Christopher Ranch Garlic**

Party Chicken Tarts

- 2 tablespoons butter or margarine
- 1 cup chopped fresh mushrooms
- ¼ cup finely chopped celery
- ¼ cup finely chopped onion
- 2 tablespoons all-purpose flour
- 1½ cups chopped cooked chicken
- 6 tablespoons sour cream
- ½ teaspoon garlic salt
- 1 package (10 ounces) flaky refrigerator biscuits (10 to 12 count)
  Vegetable cooking spray
- 1 tablespoon butter or margarine, melted
  Grated Parmesan cheese

Melt 2 tablespoons butter in large skillet until hot. Add mushrooms, celery and onion; cook and stir 4 to 5 minutes. Sprinkle with flour; stir in chicken and sour cream. Cook until thoroughly heated. Stir in garlic salt; set aside. Cut each biscuit into quarters; press each piece into miniature muffin tins coated with cooking spray to form tart shell. Brush each piece with melted butter. Bake at 400°F 6 minutes. Remove from oven; *reduce oven temperature to 350°F.* Fill each tart with 1 teaspoon chicken mixture; sprinkle with cheese. Bake 14 to 15 minutes more. Serve immediately.

Makes 40 to 48 appetizers

Note: For ease in serving at party time, prepare filling ahead and cook tarts 5 minutes. Fill and bake just before serving for best flavor.

Favorite recipe from **National Broiler Council**

Chicken Rice Roll-Ups

2 cups finely chopped cooked chicken
2 cups cooked rice
1 can (8 ounces) water chestnuts,
   drained and finely chopped
1 cup (4 ounces) grated Cheddar cheese
1 cup chopped celery
⅔ cup sour cream
½ cup finely chopped onion
1 can (4 ounces) chopped green chiles
2 teaspoons chili powder
1 teaspoon salt
¼ teaspoon hot pepper sauce
66 wonton skins
4 cups vegetable oil, for frying
   Picante sauce

Combine chicken, rice, water chestnuts, cheese, celery,
sour cream, onion, chiles, chili powder, salt and pepper
sauce in large bowl. Place 1 tablespoon rice mixture in
center of each wonton skin. Fold bottom corner up
over filling, then fold in side corners over filling. Brush
edges with water and roll up to seal. Heat oil in deep
fryer or heavy saucepan to 375°F; fry rolls, a few at a
time, 1 minute or until golden brown. Remove with
slotted spoon; drain on paper towels. Serve warm with
picante sauce for dipping.   *Makes 66 appetizers*

Favorite recipe from **USA Rice Council**

Party Chicken Sandwiches

1½ cups finely chopped cooked chicken
1 cup MIRACLE WHIP® Salad Dressing
1 (4-ounce) can chopped green chilies, drained
¾ cup (3 ounces) 100% Natural KRAFT® Shredded Sharp Cheddar Cheese
¼ cup finely chopped onion
36 party rye or pumpernickel bread slices

Combine chicken, salad dressing, chilies, cheese and onion; mix lightly. Cover bread with chicken mixture. Broil 5 minutes or until lightly browned. Serve hot. Garnish as desired.   *Makes 3 dozen sandwiches*

Variation: Substitute MIRACLE WHIP® Light Reduced Calorie Salad Dressing for Regular Salad Dressing.

Chicken Sesame with Oriental Crème

- ⅓ cup reduced sodium soy sauce
- 2 teaspoons minced garlic
- 1 teaspoon dark sesame oil
- ½ teaspoon ground ginger
- 1 pound boneless, skinless chicken breasts, cut into 4 × ½-inch strips
- 6 ounces (1 carton) ALPINE LACE® Fat Free Cream Cheese with Garlic & Herbs
- 2 tablespoons minced green onion
- 2 tablespoons sesame seeds, toasted
- 1 tablespoon extra virgin olive oil

1. To marinate the chicken: In a small bowl, whisk the soy sauce, garlic, sesame oil and ginger. Reserve 2 tablespoons and pour the remaining marinade into a self-sealing plastic bag. Add the chicken pieces and seal the bag. Turn the bag to coat all the chicken, then refrigerate 2 hours, turning bag occasionally.

2. To make Oriental Crème: In another small bowl, place cream cheese. Whisk in reserved marinade; add onion. Cover; refrigerate.

3. To prepare the chicken: Remove the chicken from the marinade and discard any remaining marinade. Spread the sesame seeds on a plate and roll the chicken strips in them until lightly coated. In a large nonstick skillet, heat the olive oil over medium-high heat. Add chicken and stir-fry 6 minutes or until golden brown and juices run clear. Serve with Oriental Crème.

Makes 24 appetizer servings

Oriental Chicken Balls

1 tablespoon butter or margarine
1 tablespoon all-purpose flour
½ cup warm milk
3 tablespoons finely chopped onion
1 cup chopped cooked chicken
1 teaspoon lemon juice
1 tablespoon chopped fresh parsley
½ teaspoon salt
⅛ teaspoon ground black pepper
⅓ cup cornstarch
  Vegetable oil, for frying
  Sweet and sour sauce

Melt butter in small skillet over medium heat until hot; stir in flour and cook until smooth and lightly browned. Slowly stir in milk until sauce is thick and smooth. Bring to a boil, stirring constantly. Stir in onion; cook about 5 minutes over low heat. Stir in chicken, lemon juice, parsley, salt and pepper; transfer to small bowl. Refrigerate until cold. Shape into 1-inch balls; keep refrigerated until ready to cook. Place cornstarch on waxed paper. Roll chicken balls in cornstarch. Heat 1 inch oil in large skillet to 375°F. Add chicken balls; cook only until light brown. Serve hot with sweet and sour sauce for dipping.

Makes 10 servings
(about 30 to 34 appetizers)

Favorite recipe from **National Broiler Council**

First

COURSES

Roasted Red Pepper Pesto Cheesecake

    1 cup butter-flavored cracker crumbs
       (about 40 crackers)
    ¼ cup (½ stick) butter or margarine
    2 packages (8 ounces *each*)
       PHILADELPHIA BRAND® Cream
       Cheese, softened
    1 cup ricotta cheese
    3 eggs
    ½ cup (2 ounces) KRAFT® 100% Grated
       Parmesan Cheese
    ½ cup DI GIORNO® Pesto Sauce
    ½ cup drained roasted red peppers, puréed

MIX crumbs and butter. Press onto bottom of 9-inch springform pan. Bake at 325°F for 10 minutes.

MIX cream cheese and ricotta cheese with electric mixer on medium speed until well blended. Add eggs, 1 at a time, mixing well after each addition. Blend in remaining ingredients. Pour over crust.

BAKE at 325°F for 55 minutes to 1 hour. Run knife or metal spatula around rim of pan to loosen cake; cool before removing rim of pan. Refrigerate 4 hours or overnight. Let stand 15 minutes at room temperature before serving. Garnish, if desired. Serve with crackers.

Makes 12 to 14 servings

Roasted Sweet Pepper Tapas

2   red bell peppers (8 ounces *each*)
1   clove garlic, minced
1   teaspoon chopped fresh oregano leaves
     or ½ teaspoon dried oregano leaves,
     crushed
2   tablespoons olive oil
     Garlic bread (optional)
     Fresh oregano sprig, for garnish

1. Preheat broiler. Broil peppers 15 to 20 minutes or until blackened on all sides, turning peppers every 5 minutes with tongs.

2. To steam peppers and loosen skin, place blackened peppers in paper bag. Close bag; set aside to cool about 15 to 20 minutes.

3. Peel peppers with paring knife. Cut in half lenthwise. Lay halves flat and slice lengthwise into ¼-inch strips.

4. Transfer pepper strips to glass jar. Add garlic, oregano and oil. Close lid; shake to blend. Marinate at least 1 hour. Serve on plates with garlic bread or refrigerate in jar up to 1 week. Garnish, if desired.

Makes 6 appetizer servings

Fruit Antipasto Platter

1 DOLE® Fresh Pineapple
2 medium, firm DOLE® Bananas, sliced
    diagonally
2 DOLE® Oranges, peeled and sliced
½ cup thinly sliced DOLE® Red Onion
½ pound low-fat sharp Cheddar cheese,
    cut into 1-inch cubes
2 jars (6 ounces *each*) marinated
    artichoke hearts, drained and halved
    DOLE® Green or Red Leaf Lettuce
½ cup fat free or light Italian salad
    dressing

• **Twist** crown from pineapple. Quarter pineapple lengthwise; remove core. Cut whole fruit from skin; slice fruit into thin wedges.

• **Arrange** pineapple, bananas, oranges, onion, cheese and artichoke hearts on lettuce-lined platter; serve with dressing. Garnish with orange zest and fresh herbs, if desired. *Makes 10 servings*

Artichokes with Dijon Mayonnaise

> 2 **DOLE® Fresh Artichokes**
>   **Lemon juice**
> ⅔ **cup fat free or reduced fat mayonnaise**
> 2 **tablespoons finely chopped DOLE®**
>   **Green Onion**
> 1 **tablespoon lemon juice**
> 1 **tablespoon Dijon mustard**
> ¼ **teaspoon prepared horseradish**

• **Wash** artichokes; trim stems. Cut 1 inch off tops of artichokes; cut off sharp leaf tips. Brush cut edges with lemon juice to prevent browning.

• **Place** artichokes in large pot of boiling water (artichokes should be completely covered with water). Cook, covered, 25 to 35 minutes or until leaf pulls off easily from artichoke. Drain artichokes upside down 10 to 15 minutes.

• **Stir** together mayonnaise, green onion, 1 tablespoon lemon juice, mustard and horseradish in small bowl until blended.

• **Spoon** dip into serving bowl. Garnish with fresh parsley, if desired. Serve with artichokes.

Makes 6 servings

Marinated Artichokes & Shrimp in Citrus Vinaigrette

VINAIGRETTE
- 1 large seedless orange, peeled and sectioned
- 3 tablespoons red wine vinegar
- 3 tablespoons fat-free mayonnaise
- 1 teaspoon fresh thyme *or* ¼ teaspoon dried thyme leaves, crushed
- 2 teaspoons extra virgin olive oil

SALAD
- 1 package (9 ounces) frozen artichoke hearts, thawed
- 12 raw shrimp (12 ounces)
- 1 cup orange juice

1. To prepare vinaigrette, combine all vinaigrette ingredients except oil in blender or food processor; blend until smooth. Pour mixture into medium nonmetal bowl and whisk in oil until blended. Fold artichoke hearts into vinaigrette. Cover and refrigerate 2 hours or overnight.

2. Peel shrimp, leaving tails attached. Devein and butterfly shrimp. Bring orange juice to a boil in medium saucepan. Add shrimp and cook about 2 minutes or just until they turn pink and opaque.

3. To serve, place about 3 artichoke hearts on each of 6 plates. Top each serving with 2 shrimp. Drizzle vinaigrette over tops. Garnish with fresh Italian parsley, if desired.   *Makes 6 appetizer servings*

Grilled Antipasto

⅔ cup A.1.® Steak Sauce
¼ cup lemon juice
2 tablespoons olive oil
1 teaspoon dried basil leaves
2 cloves garlic, minced
16 medium scallops (about ⅔ pound)
16 medium shrimp, shelled and deveined
   (about ¾ pound)
12 mushrooms
2 ounces thinly sliced cooked roast beef
   or ham
16 (2×½-inch) eggplant strips
1 (6½-ounce) jar marinated artichoke
   hearts, drained
1 red bell pepper, thickly sliced
   Lettuce leaves and lemon wedges, for
   garnish

Soak 12 (10-inch) wooden skewers in water for at least 30 minutes. In medium bowl, combine steak sauce, lemon juice, olive oil, basil and garlic; set aside.

Thread 4 scallops onto each of 4 skewers and 4 shrimp onto each of 4 skewers; thread 6 mushrooms onto each of 2 skewers. Cut roast beef or ham into 3×1-inch strips; wrap around eggplant strips and secure with wooden toothpick. Wrap remaining beef or ham around artichoke hearts; thread onto remaining 2 skewers. Place skewers, eggplant bundles and pepper slices on baking sheet; brush with steak sauce mixture.

Grill over medium heat for 7 to 10 minutes or until
seafood is opaque and vegetables are tender, turning
and basting several times. Remove each item from grill
as it is cooked; place on large lettuce-lined serving
platter. Garnish with lemon wedges, if desired.

Makes 8 appetizer servings

Stir-Fried Shrimp Appetizers

¼ **cup KIKKOMAN® Soy Sauce**
¼ **cup dry white wine**
¼ **cup chopped green onions**
1 **clove garlic, pressed**
1 **teaspoon ground ginger**
1 **pound raw medium-size shrimp, peeled**
   and deveined
3 **tablespoons vegetable oil**

Combine soy sauce, wine, green onions, garlic and
ginger. Stir in shrimp and let stand 15 minutes. Heat
oil in hot wok or large skillet over medium-high heat.
Drain shrimp and add to pan. Stir-fry 1 to 2 minutes,
or until shrimp is pink. Serve immediately.

Makes 8 appetizer servings

Surf and Turf Brochettes

  1   **(12-ounce) beef top round steak, cut
        into ¾-inch cubes**
 24   **small shrimp, peeled and deveined**
  1   **green bell pepper, cut into 1-inch
        squares**
  ¾   **cup orange juice**
  ½   **cup A.1.® Steak Sauce**
  2   **tablespoons white wine**
  1   **clove garlic, minced**
 1½   **teaspoons cornstarch**

Soak 12 (10-inch) wooden skewers in water for at least
30 minutes. Alternately thread beef cubes, shrimp and
green pepper onto skewers.

In small saucepan, combine orange juice, steak sauce,
wine and garlic; reserve ½ cup mixture for basting.
Blend cornstarch into remaining steak sauce mixture
in saucepan. Over medium heat, cook and stir until
sauce thickens and begins to boil; keep warm.

Grill brochettes over medium heat for 8 to 10 minutes
or until done, turning and brushing often with
reserved steak sauce mixture. Serve brochettes with
warm sauce for dipping.   *Makes 12 appetizers*

Scallops à la Schaller

1   **pound uncooked bacon, slices cut in
    half crosswise**
2   **pounds raw small sea scallops**
½   **cup olive oil**
½   **cup dry vermouth**
2   **tablespoons chopped fresh parsley**
1   **teaspoon garlic powder**
1   **teaspoon black pepper**
½   **teaspoon onion powder**
⅛   **teaspoon dried oregano leaves**

Wrap 1 bacon piece around each scallop; secure with
wooden toothpicks, if necessary. Place in 13×9-inch
baking dish.

Blend oil, vermouth, parsley, garlic powder, pepper,
onion powder and oregano in small bowl. Pour over
scallops; cover. Marinate in refrigerator at least
4 hours.

Remove scallops from marinade; discard marinade.
Arrange on rack of broiler pan. Broil, 4 inches from
heat, 12 to 15 minutes or until bacon is brown and
scallops are opaque, turning once. Remove toothpicks.
Arrange on lettuce-lined platter and garnish with strips
of lemon peel, if desired.   *Makes 8 servings*

Favorite recipe from **New Jersey Department of Agriculture**

Grilled Scallop Ceviche

6 to 7 ounces raw sea scallops, 1 to
   2 inches in diameter
¼ cup fresh lime juice, divided
¼ teaspoon chili powder or paprika
½ large honeydew melon
1 ripe medium papaya or mango, or
   ½ large cantaloupe
¼ cup minced onion
1 to 2 fresh jalapeño or serrano peppers,
   seeded, minced
3 tablespoons minced fresh mint or basil
1 teaspoon honey (optional)

1. Rinse scallops and pat dry. Place scallops,
2 tablespoons lime juice and chili powder in large
resealable food storage bag. Press air from bag and seal.
Marinate scallops in refrigerator 30 minutes to 1 hour.

2. Scoop seeds from melon. Remove fruit from rind
with melon baller or cut melon into ¾-inch wedges and
remove rind, then cut fruit into cubes. Cut papaya into
halves and scoop out seeds. Remove peel with knife;
cut fruit into cubes. Place fruit in nonmetallic bowl.
Stir in remaining 2 tablespoons lime juice, onion and
jalapeño. Cover and refrigerate.

3. Spray cold grid with nonstick cooking spray. Adjust
grid 4 to 6 inches above heat. Preheat grill to medium-
high heat.

4. Drain scallops; discard marinade. Thread scallops onto 10- to 12-inch metal skewers. Grill skewers 3 minutes or until marks are established. Turn skewers over; grill 3 minutes more or until scallops are opaque.

5. Remove scallops from skewers; cut into quarters. Stir into fruit mixture. Refrigerate until thoroughly chilled, about 30 minutes or up to 24 hours. Stir in mint and honey, if desired.   *Makes 6 servings*

Oysters Romano

———

   1 **dozen oysters, shucked**
   2 **slices bacon, cut into 1-inch pieces**
   ½ **cup Italian-seasoned dry bread crumbs**
   2 **tablespoons butter or margarine,**
       melted
   ½ **teaspoon garlic salt**
   6 **tablespoons grated Romano, Parmesan**
       or provolone cheese
       Fresh chives, for garnish

1. Preheat oven to 375°F. Place shells with oysters on baking sheet. Top each oyster with 1 piece bacon. Bake 10 minutes or until bacon is crisp.

2. Meanwhile, combine bread crumbs, butter and garlic salt in small bowl. Spoon mixture over oysters; top with cheese. Bake 5 to 10 minutes or until cheese melts. Serve immediately. Garnish, if desired.
     Makes 4 appetizer servings

Mini California Tuna Cakes with Remoulade Sauce

---

    3 tablespoons butter or margarine
    ½ cup minced celery
    ¼ cup minced green onions, including
       tops
    ¼ cup minced red bell pepper
    3 eggs, beaten
    1 tablespoon Dijon mustard
    ½ cup half & half or whipping cream
    3½ to 4 cups fresh bread crumbs, divided
    2 tablespoons minced fresh parsley
    1 can (12 ounces) STARKIST® Solid
       White or Chunk Light Tuna, drained
       and finely flaked
       Salt and pepper to taste
       Olive oil and butter, as needed
       Remoulade Sauce (recipe follows)

In small saucepan, melt 3 tablespoons butter over
medium heat. Add celery, onions and red pepper; sauté
until onions are soft. Cool. In large bowl, combine
eggs, mustard, half & half and sautéed vegetables; mix
well. Stir in about 3½ cups bread crumbs, parsley and
tuna; add salt and pepper. Chill at least 3 hours. Shape
into small balls, using about 2 tablespoons mixture;
flatten slightly. (If tuna mixture is too moist to shape,
add more bread crumbs.) In large skillet, heat several
tablespoons olive oil and butter over medium-high
heat until hot; sauté mini tuna cakes in batches about

1 minute per side. Remove from skillet; keep warm in 300°F oven. Serve immediately with Remoulade Sauce.

Makes 20 servings

Tip: For dinner-size tuna cakes, shape into patties 2½ inches wide and ¾ inch thick; sauté about 4 minutes per side.

Remoulade Sauce

- 1 **cup mayonnaise**
- 2 **tablespoons whole grain Dijon mustard**
- 2 **tablespoons finely chopped gherkins**
- 2 **tablespoons drained chopped capers**
- 1 **tablespoon minced fresh parsley**
- 1 **teaspoon dried tarragon, crushed**
- ½ **teaspoon freshly grated lemon peel**
- ½ **teaspoon ground black pepper**
  Salt to taste

In blender or food processor bowl with metal blade, combine all ingredients; blend well. Chill several hours before serving with Mini California Tuna Cakes.

Chilled Seafood Lasagna with Herbed Cheese

2 **cups Wisconsin Ricotta cheese**
1½ **cups Wisconsin Mascarpone cheese**
2 **tablespoons lemon juice**
1 **tablespoon minced fresh basil**
1 **tablespoon chopped fresh chives**
1 **tablespoon minced fresh dill**
1 **tablespoon minced fresh tarragon**
¼ **teaspoon white pepper**
8 **lasagna noodles (2 inches wide), cooked, drained**
1 **pound lox**
4 **ounces whitefish caviar, gently rinsed**

Place cheeses, lemon juice, herbs and pepper in food processor; process until blended. Line terrine mold with plastic wrap, allowing wrap to come over sides of pan.* Layer 1 noodle, ½ cup cheese mixture, 2 ounces lox and 2 rounded teaspoons caviar in pan. Repeat layers with remaining ingredients, ending with noodle. Cover; refrigerate several hours or until firm. Carefully remove from mold; remove plastic wrap. Garnish with strips of lox rolled to look like roses and fresh herb sprigs. Slice with warm knife.   *Makes 24 servings*

*Can be prepared without terrine mold. Layer lasagna on plastic wrap; proceed as directed. Cover; wrap with foil.

Favorite recipe from **Wisconsin Milk Marketing Board**

Tortellini Kabobs

1   cup water
⅔   cup (6-ounce can) CONTADINA® Dalla Casa Buitoni Italian Paste with Roasted Garlic
2   tablespoons CROSSE & BLACKWELL® Capers
2   tablespoons chopped fresh basil *or* 1 teaspoon dried basil, crushed
1   teaspoon Italian herb seasoning
¼   teaspoon crushed red pepper
6   cups bite-size kabob ingredients such as: cooked, drained, refrigerated CONTADINA® Dalla Casa Buitoni Tortellini, cocktail franks, smoked sausage, cooked shrimp, small fresh mushrooms, bell pepper or onion

COMBINE water, tomato paste, capers, basil, Italian herb seasoning and crushed red pepper in small saucepan. Bring to a boil. Reduce heat to low; cook, stirring occasionally, 5 to 10 minutes or until flavors are blended.

COMBINE kabob ingredients and tomato marinade in large bowl. Chill, covered, 1 hour.

THREAD kabob ingredients onto skewers; brush with any remaining marinade. Broil 5 inches from heat, 2 to 3 minutes, turning once, until heated through.

Makes 12 appetizer servings

Mediterranean Frittata

¼ cup olive oil
5 small yellow onions, thinly sliced
1 can (14½ ounces) whole peeled
      tomatoes, drained and chopped
¼ pound prosciutto or cooked ham,
      chopped
¼ cup grated Parmesan cheese
2 tablespoons chopped fresh parsley
½ teaspoon dried marjoram leaves,
      crushed
¼ teaspoon dried basil leaves, crushed
¼ teaspoon salt
    Generous dash freshly ground black
      pepper
6 eggs
2 tablespoons butter or margarine
    Italian parsley leaves, for garnish

1. Heat oil in medium skillet over medium-high heat.
Cook and stir onions in hot oil 6 to 8 minutes until soft
and golden. Add tomatoes. Cook and stir over medium
heat 5 minutes. Remove tomatoes and onions to large
bowl with slotted spoon; discard drippings. Cool
tomato-onion mixture to room temperature.

2. Stir prosciutto, cheese, parsley, marjoram, basil, salt and pepper into cooled tomato-onion mixture. Whisk eggs in small bowl; stir into prosciutto mixture.

3. Preheat broiler. Heat butter in large broiler-proof skillet over medium heat until melted and bubbly; reduce heat to low.

4. Add egg mixture to skillet, spreading evenly. Cook over low heat 8 to 10 minutes until all but top ¼ inch of egg mixture is set; shake pan gently to test. *Do not stir.*

5. Broil egg mixture about 4 inches from heat 1 to 2 minutes or until top of egg mixture is set. (Do not brown or frittata will be dry.) Frittata can be served hot, at room temperature or cold. To serve, cut into wedges. Garnish, if desired.

Makes 6 to 8 appetizer servings

Pot Stickers

    2 cups all-purpose flour
    ¾ cup plus 2 tablespoons boiling water
    ½ cup very finely chopped napa cabbage
    8 ounces lean ground pork
    2 tablespoons finely chopped water
         chestnuts
    1 green onion with top, finely chopped
   1½ teaspoons soy sauce
   1½ teaspoons dry sherry
    ½ teaspoon minced fresh ginger
   1½ teaspoons cornstarch
    ½ teaspoon sesame oil
    ¼ teaspoon sugar
    2 tablespoons vegetable oil, divided
    ⅔ cup chicken broth, divided
         Soy sauce, vinegar and chili oil

1. Place flour in large bowl; make well in center. Pour
in boiling water; stir with wooden spoon until mixture
forms dough.

2. On lightly floured surface, knead dough about
5 minutes or until smooth and satiny. Cover dough; let
rest 30 minutes.

3. For filling, squeeze cabbage to remove as much
moisture as possible; place in large bowl. Add pork,
water chestnuts, onion, soy sauce, sherry, ginger,
cornstarch, sesame oil and sugar; mix well.

4. Divide dough into two equal portions; cover one portion with plastic wrap or clean towel while working with other portion. On lightly floured surface, roll out dough to ⅛-inch thickness. Cut out 3-inch circles with round cookie cutter or top of clean empty can. Place 1 rounded teaspoon filling in center of each dough circle.

5. To shape each pot sticker, lightly moisten edges of one dough circle with water; fold in half. Starting at one end, pinch curled edges together making four pleats along edge; set dumpling down firmly, seam-side up. Cover finished dumplings while shaping remaining dumplings. (Cook dumplings immediately, refrigerate for up to 4 hours or freeze in resealable plastic bag.)

6. To cook dumplings, heat 1 tablespoon vegetable oil in large nonstick skillet over medium heat. Place ½ of pot stickers in skillet, seam-side up. (If cooking frozen dumplings, do not thaw.) Cook until bottoms are golden brown, 5 to 6 minutes.

7. Pour in ⅓ cup chicken broth; cover tightly. Reduce heat to low. Simmer until all liquid is absorbed, about 10 minutes (15 minutes if frozen). Repeat with remaining vegetable oil, dumplings and chicken broth.

8. Place pot stickers, browned-side up, on serving platter. Serve with soy sauce, vinegar and chili oil for dipping.   *Makes about 3 dozen*

Ground Turkey Chinese Spring Rolls

1   **pound Ground Turkey**
1   **large clove garlic, minced**
1½ **teaspoons minced fresh gingerroot**
2   **cups thinly sliced bok choy**
½   **cup thinly sliced green onions**
2   **tablespoons reduced-sodium soy sauce**
1   **teaspoon dry sherry or rice wine**
1   **teaspoon sesame oil**
8   **sheets phyllo pastry**
   Nonstick cooking spray

1. Preheat oven to 400°F.

2. In medium nonstick skillet, over medium-high heat, sauté turkey, garlic and ginger 4 to 5 minutes or until turkey is no longer pink. Drain thoroughly.

3. In medium bowl combine turkey mixture, bok choy, onions, soy sauce, sherry and oil.

4. On clean, dry counter, layer phyllo sheets into a stack and cut into 2 (18×7-inch) rectangles. Work with one rectangle of phyllo at a time. (Keep remaining phyllo covered with a damp cloth following package instructions.)

5. Coat rectangle of phyllo with nonstick cooking spray. On counter, arrange phyllo sheet so 7-inch side is parallel to counter edge. Place ¼ cup of turkey mixture in 5-inch strip, 1 inch away from bottom and side edges of phyllo. Fold 1-inch bottom edge of phyllo over filling and fold longer edges of phyllo toward center; roll up, jelly-roll style. Phyllo may break during rolling, but will hold filling once the roll is completed.

6. Repeat step 5 with remaining rectangles of phyllo to make remaining spring rolls. On 2 (15×10-inch) cookie sheets coated with nonstick cooking spray, place rolls, seam-side-down, and coat tops of rolls with nonstick cooking spray. Bake 14 to 16 minutes or until all surfaces of rolls are golden brown.

7. Serve immediately with Chinese mustard, hoisin sauce and additional soy sauce, if desired.

Makes 16 spring rolls

Favorite recipe from **National Turkey Federation**

Rio Grande Quesadillas

2 cups shredded cooked chicken
1 package (1.0 ounce) LAWRY'S® Taco
   Spices & Seasonings
¾ cup water
1 can (16 ounces) refried beans
6 large flour tortillas
1½ cups (6 ounces) shredded Monterey
   Jack cheese
¼ cup chopped pimiento
¼ cup chopped green onions
¼ cup chopped fresh cilantro
   Vegetable oil

In medium skillet, combine chicken, Taco Spices & Seasonings and water. Bring to a boil; reduce heat and simmer, uncovered, 15 minutes. Stir in refried beans. On half of each tortilla, spread approximately ⅓ cup of chicken-bean mixture. Layer ⅙ each of cheese, pimiento, green onions and cilantro on top. Fold each tortilla in half. In large skillet, heat a small amount of oil and quickly fry folded tortilla on each side until slightly crisp. Repeat with each folded tortilla.

Makes 6 servings

Mexicali Appetizer Meatballs

⅔ cup A.1.® Steak Sauce
⅔ cup mild, medium or hot prepared salsa
1½ pounds ground beef
1 egg
½ cup plain dry bread crumbs

In small bowl, blend steak sauce and salsa. In medium
bowl, combine beef, egg, bread crumbs and ⅓ cup
sauce mixture; shape into 32 (1¼-inch) meatballs.

Arrange meatballs in single layer in shallow baking
pan. Bake at 425°F for 12 to 15 minutes or until
meatballs are cooked through.

Serve hot meatballs with remaining sauce mixture
as a dip. *Makes 32 (1¼-inch) meatballs*

Pinto Bean & Vegetable Tortilla Stacks

¾ cup (3 ounces) skim milk mozzarella
cheese, divided
½ cup part-skim ricotta cheese
½ cup shredded carrots
¼ cup chopped radishes
6 corn tortillas (6 inches each)
1 cup GUILTLESS GOURMET® Pinto
Bean Dip (mild or spicy)
Green or red bell pepper rings
(optional)
½ cup GUILTLESS GOURMET® Salsa
(mild, medium or hot)

Preheat oven to 375°F. Combine ½ cup mozzarella
cheese, ricotta cheese, carrots and radishes in small
bowl; stir well. Set aside.

Place 2 tortillas on ungreased baking sheet. Spread
each with ¼ cup bean dip; top each with ¼ of cheese
mixture. Place 1 tortilla on top of each. Spread each
tortilla with ¼ cup bean dip and ¼ of cheese mixture.
Top each with remaining 2 tortillas. Sprinkle
remaining ¼ cup mozzarella cheese evenly over stacks.

Bake 15 minutes or until thoroughly heated. Cut each
tortilla stack into quarters. Garnish with pepper rings,
if desired. Serve hot with salsa.   *Makes 8 servings*

Thai Lamb & Couscous Rolls

16 large napa or Chinese cabbage leaves,
     stems trimmed
 2 tablespoons minced fresh ginger
 1 teaspoon crushed red pepper
⅔ cup uncooked quick-cooking couscous
½ pound ground lean lamb
½ cup chopped green onions
 3 cloves garlic, minced
¼ cup plus 2 tablespoons chopped fresh
     cilantro or mint, divided
 2 tablespoons reduced-sodium soy sauce
 1 tablespoon lime juice
 1 teaspoon Oriental sesame oil
 1 cup plain nonfat yogurt

Place 4 cups water in medium saucepan; bring to a boil
over high heat. Drop cabbage leaves into water; cook
30 seconds. Drain. Rinse leaves under cold water until
cool; pat dry with paper towels. Place 1 cup water,
ginger and red pepper in medium saucepan; bring to a
boil over high heat. Stir in couscous; cover. Remove
saucepan from heat; let stand 5 minutes.

Spray large saucepan with nonstick cooking spray; add
lamb, onions and garlic. Cook and stir over medium-
high heat 5 minutes or until lamb is no longer pink.
Combine couscous, lamb, ¼ cup cilantro, soy sauce,
lime juice and oil in medium bowl. Spoon evenly over
centers of cabbage leaves. Fold ends of cabbage leaves
over filling; roll up. Combine yogurt and remaining
2 tablespoons cilantro in small bowl; spoon evenly over
rolls. Serve warm.   *Makes 16 appetizers*

Snappy

SNACKS

Sesame Cheese Crackers

- 1 cup all-purpose flour
- ½ teaspoon salt
- ⅛ teaspoon ground red pepper (cayenne)
- 6 tablespoons cold butter or margarine
- 1 cup (4 ounces) finely grated Cheddar cheese
- ¼ cup sesame seed, toasted
- 4½ to 7½ teaspoons ice-cold water
- ½ teaspoon KIKKOMAN® Soy Sauce

Combine flour, salt and red pepper in medium bowl; cut in butter until mixture resembles coarse crumbs. Stir in cheese and sesame seed. Combine 3 teaspoons water and soy sauce; stir into dry ingredients. Add more water, a little at a time, mixing lightly until dough begins to stick together. Turn out dough and press together on lightly floured board or pastry cloth; roll out to ⅛-inch thickness. Cut dough into 2×1-inch rectangles with pastry wheel or knife. Place on lightly greased baking sheets and bake in 400°F oven 8 to 10 minutes or until lightly browned. Remove crackers to rack to cool.   *Makes 8 appetizer servings*

Cheddar Wafers

1½ cups (6 ounces) shredded ALPINE
      LACE® Fat Free Pasteurized Process
      Skim Milk Cheese Product—For
      Cheddar Lovers
¼ cup butter, softened
3 tablespoons vegetable oil
1¼ cups unsifted all-purpose flour
½ teaspoon salt
½ teaspoon dry mustard
¼ teaspoon cayenne pepper

1. In the bowl of a food processor, process the cheese and butter for about 30 seconds or until combined. With the machine running, slowly pour the oil through the feed tube.

2. Add the flour, salt, mustard and pepper. Process for 30 seconds or just until the mixture resembles coarse crumbs. *(Avoid overprocessing!)* Remove the dough, shape into a ball, wrap in plastic wrap and refrigerate for 30 minutes.

3. Preheat the oven to 350°F. Shape the dough into 30 (¾-inch) balls and place them 2 inches apart on 2 baking sheets.

4. Using the tines of a fork, slightly flatten each ball in a crisscross pattern until it resembles a coin that is ⅛ inch thick. Bake for 15 minutes or just until crisp, but not browned. Transfer wafers to wire racks, dust lightly with paprika and cool. Store in an airtight container. *Makes 2½ dozen wafers*

Pita Chips

½ cup (1 stick) butter or margarine,
   melted
1 envelope GOOD SEASONS® Italian
   Salad Dressing Mix
4 large pita breads, split

MIX butter and salad dressing mix in small bowl until
well blended. Brush or drizzle on pita bread rounds.
Cut each pita bread round into 4 wedges. Arrange in
single layer on cookie sheets.

BAKE at 350°F for 10 to 12 minutes or until crisp.

Makes 32 chips

Steak Nachos

1 (1-pound) beef top round steak,
     chopped
¼ cup chopped onion
1 tablespoon vegetable oil
½ cup A.1.® ORIGINAL Steak Sauce
5 cups tortilla chips
2 cups (8 ounces) shredded Cheddar or
     Monterey Jack cheese
1 cup chopped fresh tomatoes
¼ cup diced green chiles or jalapeño
     pepper slices
¼ cup sliced pitted ripe olives
   Sour cream (optional)

In large skillet, over medium-high heat, sauté steak
and onion in oil until steak is no longer pink; drain.
Stir in steak sauce. Arrange tortilla chips on large
heatproof platter or baking sheet. Spoon steak mixture
over chips; sprinkle with cheese. Broil 6 inches from
heat source 3 to 5 minutes or until cheese melts. Top
with tomatoes, chiles and olives. Serve immediately
with sour cream, on the side, if desired.

Makes 6 appetizer servings

Spam™ Nachos

1 (10½-ounce) bag CHI–CHI'S® Tortilla
   Chips
1 (12-ounce) can SPAM® Luncheon Meat,
   cubed
1 (16-ounce) jar CHI–CHI'S® Salsa
1 (15-ounce) can CHI–CHI'S® Refried
   Beans
1 (8-ounce) package shredded Mexican
   pasteurized processed cheese

Heat oven to 425°F. Place chips on baking sheet.
Sprinkle SPAM® over chips. In medium bowl, combine
salsa and refried beans; pour over chips. Sprinkle with
cheese. Bake 6 to 7 minutes or until cheese is melted.
Serve immediately. *Makes 10 appetizer servings*

Ham and Gouda Quesadilla Snacks

1½ cups shredded smoked Gouda cheese
(6 ounces)
1 cup chopped ham (4 ounces)
½ cup pitted ripe olives, chopped
¼ cup minced red onion
½ cup GREY POUPON® COUNTRY
DIJON® Mustard
8 (6- or 7-inch) flour tortillas
Sour cream, chopped bell peppers,
sliced pitted ripe olives and cilantro,
for garnish

In small bowl, combine cheese, ham, olives and onion.
Spread 1 tablespoon mustard on each tortilla; spread
about ⅓ cup cheese mixture over half of each tortilla.
Fold tortilla in half to cover filling.

In large nonstick skillet, over medium heat, heat filled
tortillas for 4 minutes or until cheese melts, turning
once. Cut each quesadilla into 3 wedges. Place on
serving platter; garnish with sour cream, peppers,
olives and cilantro.   *Makes 24 appetizers*

Antipasto Mini Pizzas

1¾ cups (14.5-ounce can) CONTADINA®
     Dalla Casa Buitoni Original Chunky
     Pizza Sauce
¾ cup (6-ounce jar) marinated artichoke
     hearts, drained, coarsely chopped
½ cup chopped green bell pepper
½ cup (2¼-ounce can) sliced ripe olives,
     drained
2 tablespoons grated Parmesan cheese
6 plain bagels, sliced horizontally, lightly
     toasted
1 cup (4 ounces) grated mozzarella
     cheese

COMBINE pizza sauce, artichoke hearts, bell pepper, olives and Parmesan cheese in medium bowl. Spoon pizza sauce mixture onto bagel halves. Sprinkle with mozzarella cheese.

BAKE in preheated 400°F oven for 6 to 8 minutes or until heated through.   *Makes 6 servings*

Teriyaki Nut Nibbles

1   cup whole natural almonds
¼   cup KIKKOMAN® Teriyaki Sauce
2   tablespoons water
2   teaspoons brown sugar, packed
1½ cups dry roasted unsalted peanuts
¾   teaspoon vegetable oil

Preheat oven to 350°F. Toast almonds on ungreased
baking sheet 10 minutes; do not stir. Remove; cool in
pan on wire rack. *Reduce oven temperature to 250°F.*
Combine teriyaki sauce, water and brown sugar in
1-quart saucepan. Bring to boil over medium-low heat.
Stir in almonds and peanuts; boil 5 minutes, or until
sauce is absorbed by nuts, stirring frequently. Add oil
and toss nuts until coated; turn onto baking sheet,
separating nuts. Bake in 250°F oven 7 minutes. Shake
and turn nuts; bake 7 minutes longer. Remove nuts
from pan and cool in single layer. Store in tightly
covered container.   *Makes 2½ cups*

Teri Snack Mix

⅓ cup KIKKOMAN® Teriyaki Sauce
2 tablespoons vegetable oil
1 cup pecan halves
1 cup walnut halves
2 cups toasted oat cereal
1 cup shredded coconut
¾ cup sunflower seed
½ cup slivered blanched almonds
1 cup raisins

Combine teriyaki sauce and oil in large bowl; stir in pecans and walnuts until thoroughly coated. Let stand 10 minutes, stirring occasionally. Add cereal, coconut, sunflower seed and almonds; toss together to combine and coat thoroughly. Turn onto large shallow baking pan, spreading mixture out evenly. Bake in 250°F oven 15 minutes. Remove from oven; stir gently. Bake 15 minutes longer. Remove from oven and stir in raisins. Let stand in pan until cooled thoroughly. Store in tightly covered container.   *Makes about 6 cups*

Southwest Snack Mix

4 **cups corn cereal squares**
2 **cups unsalted pretzels**
½ **cup unsalted pumpkin or squash seeds**
1½ **teaspoons chili powder**
1 **teaspoon minced cilantro leaves or parsley**
½ **teaspoon garlic powder**
½ **teaspoon onion powder**
1 **egg white**
2 **tablespoons olive oil**
2 **tablespoons lime juice**

1. Preheat oven to 300°F. Spray large nonstick baking sheet with nonstick cooking spray.

2. Combine cereal, pretzels and pumpkin seeds in large bowl. Combine chili powder, cilantro, garlic powder and onion powder in small bowl.

3. Whisk together egg white, oil and lime juice in separate small bowl. Pour over cereal mixture; toss to coat evenly. Add seasoning mixture; mix lightly to coat evenly. Transfer to prepared baking sheet.

4. Bake 45 minutes, stirring every 15 minutes; cool. Store in airtight container.

Makes 12 (½-cup) servings

Smokey Grey Poupon® Bridge Mix

1 (12-ounce) can PLANTERS® Unsalted
   Mixed Nuts
⅓ cup GREY POUPON® Dijon Mustard
2 tablespoons margarine or butter, melted
¾ teaspoon WRIGHT'S® Natural Hickory
   Seasoning
½ teaspoon garlic powder
1 cup sesame sticks

Place mixed nuts in shallow baking pan. Bake at 300°F
for 20 minutes, stirring occasionally.

In medium bowl, blend mustard, margarine or butter,
hickory seasoning and garlic powder. Stir in hot nuts
until coated. Return coated nuts to baking pan. Bake at
300°F for 20 to 25 minutes or until nuts are browned
and slightly dry. Stir in sesame sticks; cool. Store in
airtight container.   *Makes about 3 cups mix*

Pizza Snack Mix

2   quarts popped popcorn
1   cup sesame sticks
1   cup pretzel or plain goldfish crackers
1   cup unsalted peanuts
½   cup grated Parmesan cheese
½   cup butter or margarine
1   package (1.1 ounces) HIDDEN
      VALLEY RANCH® Ranch Italian salad
      dressing mix
1   tablespoon Worcestershire sauce
2   teaspoons dried oregano, crushed
1   teaspoon dry mustard
½   teaspoon crushed red pepper (optional)

Preheat oven to 300°F. In large bowl, combine
popcorn, sesame sticks, crackers, peanuts and cheese.
In small saucepan, melt butter over low heat. Stir in
salad dressing mix, Worcestershire sauce, oregano,
mustard and red pepper, if desired, to blend. Slowly
pour over mixture in bowl, tossing to coat evenly.
Spread in shallow baking pan; bake 15 to 20 minutes,
stirring occasionally. Cool; store in airtight container.

Makes about 10 cups mix

Original Crispix® Mix

7 cups KELLOGG'S® CRISPIX® cereal
1 cup mixed nuts
1 cup pretzels
3 tablespoons margarine, melted
¼ teaspoon garlic salt
¼ teaspoon onion salt
2 teaspoons lemon juice
4 teaspoons Worcestershire sauce

1. Preheat oven to 250°F. Combine KELLOGG'S® CRISPIX® cereal, nuts and pretzels in 13×9-inch baking pan. Set aside.

2. Stir together remaining ingredients. Gently stir into cereal mixture until evenly coated.

3. Bake at 250°F about 45 minutes, stirring every 15 minutes. Spread on paper towels to cool. Store in airtight container.   *Makes 9 cups mix*

Microwave Directions: In large microwave-safe bowl, combine cereal, nuts and pretzels. Follow step 2 above. Microwave at HIGH (100% power) 4 minutes, stirring after 2 minutes. Spread on paper towels to cool. Store in airtight container. (These microwave directions were tested in a 700-watt microwave oven. Cooking times may vary depending on microwave oven.)

Oriental Snack Mix

¼ **cup butter**
4 **cups corn or rice cereal squares**
1 **cup honey roasted peanuts**
1 **can (5 ounces) chow mein noodles**
3 **tablespoons teriyaki sauce**
1 **tablespoon dark sesame oil**
1 **teaspoon garlic powder**

1. Preheat oven to 250°F. Grease 13×9-inch baking pan. Set aside.

2. To melt butter, place butter in 2-cup glass measure. Microwave at MEDIUM (50% power) 1 minute or until butter is melted. Let stand 2 minutes.

3. Combine cereal, peanuts and noodles in medium bowl. Add teriyaki sauce, oil and garlic powder to glass measure; whisk with fork until well blended.

4. Drizzle butter mixture evenly over cereal mixture; stir with wooden spoon until evenly coated. Spread mixture in single layer in prepared baking pan.

5. Bake 1 hour or until mix is lightly browned, stirring every 15 minutes with wooden spoon. Cool completely in pan on wire rack.

6. Store in airtight container at room temperature up to 2 weeks.   *Makes 6 cups mix*

Chex® brand Party Mix

¼ **cup margarine or butter**
5 **teaspoons Worcestershire sauce**
1¼ **teaspoons seasoned salt**
¼ **teaspoon garlic powder**
2⅔ **cups Corn CHEX® brand cereal**
2⅔ **cups Rice CHEX® brand cereal**
2⅔ **cups Wheat CHEX® brand cereal**
1 **cup mixed nuts**
1 **cup pretzels**

1. Melt margarine in open roasting pan in preheated 250°F oven. Stir in seasonings.

2. Gradually add cereals, nuts and pretzels; stir to coat evenly.

3. Bake 1 hour, stirring every 15 minutes. Spread on paper towels to cool. Store in airtight container.

Makes 10 cups mix

Mexi Chex®

¼ cup margarine or butter
1 package (1.25 ounces) taco seasoning
    mix, divided
4½ cups Corn CHEX® brand cereal
1 pound ground beef
1 small head lettuce, shredded
2 medium tomatoes, chopped
1½ cups (6 ounces) shredded Cheddar
    cheese
    Salsa
    Sour cream

1. Melt margarine in microwave-safe bowl on HIGH 45 to 60 seconds. Stir in ½ package (2 tablespoons) seasoning mix. Add cereal, stirring until all pieces are evenly coated. Microwave on HIGH 2 minutes, stirring every minute.

2. Brown ground beef in large skillet over medium-high heat; drain. Stir in remaining ½ package seasoning mix and ¼ cup water. Simmer 5 minutes, stirring occasionally.

3. Layer 4 cups cereal, ground beef, lettuce, tomatoes and cheese in serving dish. Top with remaining ½ cup cereal. Serve with salsa and sour cream.

Makes 6 to 8 servings

Mexicali Crunch

- 4   cups corn flakes
- 2   quarts popped corn
- 3   cups corn or tortilla chips
- 1   cup roasted peanuts
- ½   cup (1 stick) MAZOLA® Margarine
- ½   cup KARO® Light or Dark Corn Syrup
- ¼   cup packed brown sugar
- 1   package (1.25 ounces) taco seasoning
     mix

1. Preheat oven to 250°F. In large roasting pan combine corn flakes, popped corn, corn chips and peanuts; set aside.

2. In medium saucepan combine margarine, corn syrup, brown sugar and taco seasoning. Bring to boil over medium heat, stirring constantly. Pour over corn flake mixture; toss to coat well.

3. Bake 1 hour, stirring every 15 minutes. Cool, stirring frequently. Store in tightly covered container.

Makes about 4 quarts

Honey-Roasted Bridge Mix

½ cup honey
2 tablespoons butter or margarine
1 teaspoon ground cinnamon, divided
4 cups mixed nuts
2 to 3 tablespoons superfine sugar

Preheat oven to 325°F. Combine honey, butter and
½ teaspoon cinnamon in saucepan. Bring mixture to a
boil; cook 2 minutes, stirring constantly. Pour honey
mixture over nuts; stir well until nuts are coated.
Spread nut mixture onto foil-lined cookie sheet or
jelly-roll pan.

Bake 10 to 15 minutes or until nuts are glazed and
lightly browned. *Do not allow nuts to burn.* Cool 20 to
30 minutes; remove from foil. Combine sugar and
remaining ½ teaspoon cinnamon; toss with glazed nuts
to coat.   *Makes 4 cups mix*

Favorite recipe from **National Honey Board**

Taco Popcorn Olé

8 cups air-popped popcorn
  Butter-flavored nonstick cooking spray
1 teaspoon chili powder
½ teaspoon salt
½ teaspoon garlic powder
⅛ teaspoon ground red pepper (optional)

1. Preheat oven to 350°F. Line 15×10-inch jelly-roll pan with foil.

2. Place popcorn in single layer in prepared pan. Coat lightly with cooking spray.

3. Combine chili powder, salt, garlic powder and red pepper, if desired, in small bowl; sprinkle over popcorn. Mix lightly to evenly coat.

4. Bake 5 minutes or until hot, stirring gently after 3 minutes.

5. Spread mixture in single layer on large sheet of foil to cool.   *Makes 8 (1-cup) servings*

Honey Popcorn Clusters

Vegetable cooking spray
6 cups air-popped popcorn
⅔ cup DOLE® Golden or Seedless Raisins
½ cup DOLE® Chopped Dates or Pitted
    Dates, chopped
⅓ cup DOLE® Slivered Almonds
    (optional)
⅓ cup packed brown sugar
¼ cup honey
2 tablespoons margarine
¼ teaspoon baking soda

• **Line** bottom and sides of 13×9-inch baking pan with large sheet of aluminum foil. Spray foil with vegetable cooking spray.

• **Stir** together popcorn, raisins, dates and almonds, if desired, in foil-lined pan.

• **Combine** brown sugar, honey and margarine in small saucepan. Bring to boil over medium heat, stirring constantly; reduce heat to low. Cook 5 minutes *(do not stir)*. Remove from heat.

• **Stir** in baking soda. Pour evenly over popcorn mixture, stirring quickly to coat mixture evenly.

• **Bake** at 300°F 12 to 15 minutes or until mixture is lightly browned, stirring halfway through baking time.

• **Lift** foil from pan; place on cooling rack. Cool popcorn mixture completely; break into clusters. Popcorn can be kept in airtight container for 1 week.

Makes 7 cups

Honey Pecan Mix

Vegetable cooking spray
6 cups KELLOGG'S® CRISPIX® cereal
1 cup mini-pretzel twists
1 cup pecan halves
⅓ cup margarine
¾ cup firmly packed brown sugar
¼ cup honey
1 teaspoon vanilla

1. Preheat oven to 250°F. In 13×9×2-inch baking pan coated with cooking spray, combine KELLOGG'S® CRISPIX® cereal, pretzels and pecans. Set aside.

2. In large saucepan over medium heat, combine margarine, sugar and honey. Bring to a boil and continue to boil 5 minutes. Do not stir. Remove from heat and stir in vanilla. Pour syrup over cereal mixture, stirring until well coated.

3. Bake at 250°F about 1 hour, stirring every 15 minutes. Let cool on cookie sheets. Store in airtight container.   *Makes 9 cups*

Cinnamon Trail Mix

2 cups corn cereal squares
2 cups whole wheat cereal squares or
   whole wheat cereal squares with mini
   graham crackers
1½ cups fat-free oyster crackers
½ cup broken sesame snack sticks
2 tablespoons margarine or butter, melted
1 teaspoon ground cinnamon
¼ teaspoon ground nutmeg
½ cup bite-sized fruit-flavored candy
   pieces

1. Preheat oven to 350°F. Spray 13×9-inch baking pan with nonstick cooking spray.

2. Place cereals, oyster crackers and sesame sticks in prepared pan; mix lightly.

3. Combine margarine, cinnamon and nutmeg in small bowl; mix well. Drizzle evenly over cereal mixture; toss to evenly coat.

4. Bake 12 to 14 minutes or until golden brown, stirring gently after 6 minutes. Cool completely. Stir in candies.   *Makes 8 (¾-cup) servings*

Easy Italian No-Bake Snack Mix

3 tablespoons olive oil
1 tablespoon Italian seasoning
1 box (7 ounces) baked crispy snack
    crackers
4 cups small pretzels
1 can (12 ounces) cocktail peanuts
¼ cup grated Parmesan cheese

1. Combine oil and seasoning in large resealable plastic food storage bag; knead well.

2. Add crackers, pretzels and peanuts. Seal bag; shake gently to coat well with oil mixture. Add grated cheese. Seal bag; shake gently to combine. Snack mix can be stored in bag up to 5 days.   *Makes 10 cups*

Brontosaurus Bites

4 cups air-popped popcorn
2 cups mini-dinosaur grahams
2 cups corn cereal squares
1½ cups dried pineapple wedges
1 package (6 ounces) dried fruit bits
  Butter-flavored nonstick cooking spray
1 tablespoon plus 1½ teaspoons sugar
1½ teaspoons ground cinnamon
½ teaspoon ground nutmeg
1 cup yogurt-covered raisins

1. Preheat oven to 350°F. Combine popcorn, grahams, cereal, pineapple and fruit bits in large bowl; mix lightly. Transfer to 15×10-inch jelly-roll pan. Spray mixture generously with cooking spray.

2. Combine sugar, cinnamon and nutmeg in small bowl. Sprinkle ½ of the sugar mixture over popcorn mixture; toss lightly to coat. Spray mixture again with additional cooking spray. Add remaining sugar mixture; mix lightly.

3. Bake snack mix 10 minutes, stirring after 5 minutes. Cool completely in pan on wire rack. Add raisins; mix lightly.   *Makes 12 (¾-cup) servings*

Gorilla Grub: Substitute plain raisins for the yogurt-covered raisins and ¼ cup grated Parmesan cheese for the sugar, cinnamon and nutmeg mixture.

Deviled Mixed Nuts

3 tablespoons vegetable oil
2 cups assorted unsalted nuts, such as
     peanuts, almonds, Brazil nuts or
     walnuts
2 tablespoons sugar
1 teaspoon paprika
½ teaspoon chili powder
½ teaspoon curry powder
½ teaspoon ground cumin
½ teaspoon ground coriander
½ teaspoon ground black pepper
¼ teaspoon salt

Heat oil in large skillet over medium heat; cook and
stir nuts in hot oil 2 to 3 minutes until browned.
Combine remaining ingredients in small bowl; sprinkle
over nuts. Stir to coat evenly. Heat 1 to 2 minutes
more. Drain nuts on wire rack lined with paper towels.
Serve warm.   *Makes 6 to 8 servings (2 cups)*

Hearty

SOUPS

Butternut Bisque

1 medium butternut squash (about
  1½ pounds)
1 teaspoon margarine or butter
1 large onion, coarsely chopped
2 cans (about 14 ounces *each*) reduced-
  sodium or regular chicken broth,
  divided
½ teaspoon ground nutmeg or freshly
  grated nutmeg
⅛ teaspoon ground white pepper
  Plain nonfat yogurt and chives, for
  garnish

1. Remove skin from squash with vegetable peeler. Cut squash lengthwise in half; discard seeds. Cut flesh into ½-inch pieces; set aside.

2. Melt margarine in large saucepan over medium heat. Add onion. Cook and stir 3 minutes.

3. Add 1 can broth and squash. Bring to a boil over high heat. Reduce heat to low. Cover and simmer 20 minutes or until squash is very tender.

4. Process squash mixture, in 2 batches, in food processor until smooth. Return soup to saucepan; add remaining can of broth, nutmeg and pepper. Simmer, uncovered, 5 minutes, stirring occasionally. Ladle into soup bowls. Place yogurt in pastry bag fitted with round decorating tip. Pipe onto soup in decorative design. Garnish with chives.

Makes 6 servings (about 5 cups)

Broccoli Bisque

- 1 **cup sliced broccoli flowerets**
- ¼ **cup chopped onion**
- 1½ **cups water***
- 2 **cups prepared HIDDEN VALLEY RANCH® Original Ranch® salad dressing**
- 2 **tablespoons all-purpose flour**
- ¼ **cup shredded Monterey Jack cheese (optional)**

In medium saucepan, cook broccoli and onion in water until tender, 6 to 7 minutes. In small bowl, whisk together salad dressing and flour. Add to broccoli and onion mixture. Cook over low heat until heated through. Sprinkle with cheese, if desired. Serve hot.

Serves 3 to 4

*For a richer bisque, substitute milk for water.

Creamy Vegetable Bisque

1   bag (16 ounces) BIRDS EYE® frozen
     Broccoli Cuts
2   teaspoons butter or margarine
⅓   cup chopped celery or onion
     (or a combination)
1   can (10¾ ounces) cream of celery soup
1¼ cups milk or water
1   tablespoon chopped parsley

• Cook broccoli according to package directions.

• Melt butter in saucepan. Add celery; cook and stir
3 to 5 minutes.

• Blend in broccoli, soup, milk and parsley; cook over
medium heat 4 to 5 minutes.

Makes 4 to 6 servings

Chicken Cilantro Bisque

2½ cups chicken broth
6 ounces boneless skinless chicken breast meat, cut into chunks
½ cup fresh cilantro leaves
½ cup sliced green onions
¼ cup sliced celery
1 large clove garlic, finely chopped
½ teaspoon ground cumin
⅓ cup all-purpose flour
1½ cups (12-fluid-ounce can) CARNATION® Evaporated Skimmed Milk
Salt and freshly ground black pepper to taste
Garnishes: chopped tomatoes, onions and bell peppers

Combine broth, chicken, cilantro, green onions, celery, garlic and cumin in large saucepan. Bring to a boil. Reduce heat to low; cover. Cook 15 minutes. Pour into blender container; add flour. Cover; blend until smooth.

Pour mixture back into saucepan. Cook over medium heat, stirring constantly, 8 to 10 minutes or until mixture comes to a boil and is thickened. Remove from heat. Gradually stir in evaporated milk; reheat just to serving temperature (do not boil). Season with salt and pepper. Garnish, if desired.

Makes about 4 servings

Ranch Clam Chowder

¼ **cup chopped onion**
3 **tablespoons butter or margarine**
½ **pound fresh mushrooms, sliced**
2 **tablespoons Worcestershire sauce**
1 **can (10¾ ounces) cream of potato soup**
¼ **cup dry white wine**
1½ **cups half-and-half**
1 **package (1 ounce) HIDDEN VALLEY RANCH® Milk Recipe Original Ranch® salad dressing mix**
1 **can (10 ounces) whole baby clams, undrained**
   Chopped parsley

In 3-quart saucepan, cook onion in butter over medium heat until onion is soft but not browned. Add mushrooms and Worcestershire sauce. Cook until mushrooms are soft and pan juices have almost evaporated. In medium bowl, whisk together potato soup, wine, half-and-half and salad dressing mix until smooth. Drain clam liquid into dressing mixture; stir into mushrooms in pan. Cook, uncovered, until soup is heated through but not boiling. Add clams to soup; cook until heated through. Garnish each serving with parsley.   *Makes 6 servings*

Albacore Corn Chowder

2 **tablespoons butter or margarine**
½ **cup sliced celery**
½ **cup chopped onion**
¾ **cup chopped carrot**
2 **to 3 tablespoons all-purpose flour**
1 **teaspoon dried thyme or Italian**
   seasoning
1 **can (17 ounces) cream-style corn**
2 **cups milk**
1 **can (12 ounces) STARKIST® Solid**
   White Tuna, drained and flaked
1 **cup water**
1 **teaspoon chicken flavor instant bouillon**

In medium saucepan, melt butter over medium heat; sauté celery, onion and carrot about 3 minutes. Add flour and thyme; blend well. Cook 3 more minutes. Add corn, milk, tuna, water and bouillon, stirring to blend. Cover and simmer *(do not boil)* 5 minutes to heat through, stirring occasionally. *Makes 4 servings*

Baja Corn Chowder

¼ cup butter or margarine
3 cans (17 ounces *each*) whole kernel
   corn, drained, divided
1 medium red bell pepper, diced
2 cups chicken broth
1 quart half-and-half
1 can (7 ounces) diced green chiles,
   drained
1 package (1.27 ounces) LAWRY'S®
   Spices & Seasonings for Fajitas
2 cups (8 ounces) shredded Monterey
   Jack cheese
½ teaspoon LAWRY'S® Seasoned Pepper
   Hot pepper sauce to taste

In Dutch oven or large saucepan, melt butter. Add one can corn and bell pepper; sauté 5 minutes. Remove from heat. In food processor or blender, place remaining two cans corn and chicken broth; process until smooth. Add to Dutch oven with half-and-half, chiles and Spices & Seasonings for Fajitas. Return to heat. Bring just to a boil, stirring constantly. Remove from heat; blend in cheese, Seasoned Pepper and hot pepper sauce.　　　　*Makes 4 to 6 servings*

Nacho Cheese Soup

1 package (about 5 ounces) dry au gratin
   potatoes
1 can (about 15 ounces) whole kernel
   corn, undrained
2 cups water
1 cup salsa
2 cups milk
1½ cups (6 ounces) SARGENTO® Classic
   Shredded Cheese For Tacos
1 can (about 2 ounces) sliced ripe olives,
   drained
   Tortilla chips (optional)

In large saucepan, combine potatoes, dry au gratin
sauce mix, corn with liquid, water and salsa. Heat to
a boil; reduce heat. Cover and simmer 25 minutes or
until potatoes are tender, stirring occasionally. Add
milk, taco cheese and olives. Cook until cheese is
melted and soup is heated through, stirring
occasionally. Garnish with tortilla chips.

Makes 6 servings

Potato-Cheese Calico Soup

1   pound potatoes, peeled and thinly sliced
1   cup sliced onion
2½ cups chicken broth
½   cup low-fat milk
1   cup sliced mushrooms
½   cup diced red bell pepper
½   cup sliced green onions
1   cup (4 ounces) finely shredded
       Wisconsin Asiago Cheese
    Salt and black pepper (optional)
2   tablespoons chopped fresh parsley

In 3-quart saucepan, combine potatoes, 1 cup onion
and broth. Bring to a boil. Reduce heat to low. Cover;
cook until potatoes are tender, about 10 minutes.
Transfer to blender container; blend until smooth.
Return to saucepan. Stir in milk, mushrooms, bell
pepper and green onions. Bring to a simmer over
medium-low heat. Add cheese, a few tablespoons at a
time, stirring to melt. Season with salt and black
pepper. Sprinkle with parsley.

Makes 6 (1-cup) servings

Favorite recipe from **Wisconsin Milk Marketing Board**

Creamy Asparagus Potato Soup

1   can (12 ounces) DEL MONTE®
    FreshCut™ Asparagus Spears, drained
1   can (14½ ounces) DEL MONTE
    FreshCut™ Whole New Potatoes,
    drained
½   teaspoon dried thyme, crushed
⅛   teaspoon garlic powder
1   can (14 ounces) chicken broth
1   cup milk or half & half

1. Place asparagus, potatoes, thyme and garlic powder in food processor or blender (in batches, if needed); process until smooth.

2. Pour into medium saucepan; add broth. Bring to boil. Stir in milk; heat through. *(Do not boil.)* Season with salt and pepper to taste, if desired. Serve hot or cold. Thin with additional milk or water, if desired.

Makes 4 servings

Creamy Carrot Soup

- 3 cups water
- 1 chicken bouillon cube
- 4 cups sliced carrots
- 1 Golden Delicious apple, peeled and cubed
- 2 tablespoons firmly packed brown sugar
- 2 teaspoons curry powder
  Dash ground cinnamon
- 2 tablespoons low-fat plain yogurt

In medium saucepan, combine water and bouillon cube; bring to a boil. Set broth aside. In large saucepan, using folding metal steamer or colander, steam carrots and apple for 15 minutes or until very tender. Remove from heat.

In large blender container, process carrots and apple with broth until smooth. Pour into large bowl. Stir in sugar, curry powder and cinnamon. Cover; refrigerate at least 1 hour before serving. Pour into bowls; top each serving with dollop of yogurt. Garnish as desired.

Makes 6 servings

Favorite recipe from **The Sugar Association, Inc.**

Creamy Tomatillo Soup

1 cup finely chopped onion
1 cup finely chopped celery
2 cloves garlic, minced
1 tablespoon soft margarine
¼ cup all-purpose flour
1 can (14.5 ounces) low sodium chicken broth, defatted
2 cups skim milk
1 jar (11.5 ounces) GUILTLESS GOURMET® Green Tomatillo Salsa
  Tomatillo slices and red chili pepper strips (optional)
¾ cup crushed GUILTLESS GOURMET® Unsalted Baked Tortilla Chips

Microwave Directions: Combine onion, celery, garlic and margarine in 2-quart glass measure or microwave-safe casserole. Cover with vented plastic wrap or lid; microwave on HIGH (100% power) 5 to 6 minutes or until vegetables are crisp-tender. Stir in flour. Gradually stir in broth and milk until well blended. Microwave on HIGH 10 minutes more or until slightly thickened, stirring every 3 minutes. Blend in tomatillo salsa; microwave on HIGH 1 minute more or until heated through. To serve, ladle soup into 6 individual soup bowls, dividing evenly. Garnish with tomatillo and pepper, if desired. Top each with 2 tablespoons tortilla chips.   *Makes 6 servings*

Stove Top Directions: Heat margarine in 2-quart saucepan over medium-high heat until bubbly. Add onion, celery and garlic; cook and stir until vegetables are crisp-tender. Remove from heat and stir in flour. Gradually stir in broth and milk until well blended. Bring to a boil over medium heat. Reduce heat to low; simmer until slightly thickened. Blend in tomatillo salsa and simmer 1 minute more or until heated through. Serve as directed.

Country Bean Soup

1¼ cups dried navy beans or lima beans,
    rinsed and drained
4 ounces salt pork or fully cooked ham,
    chopped
¼ cup chopped onion
½ teaspoon dried oregano leaves
¼ teaspoon salt
¼ teaspoon ground ginger
¼ teaspoon dried sage leaves
¼ teaspoon ground black pepper
2 cups skim milk
2 tablespoons butter

Place navy beans in large saucepan; add enough water
to cover beans. Bring to a boil. Reduce heat; simmer 2
minutes. Remove from heat; cover and let stand for 1
hour. (Or, cover beans with water and soak overnight.)

Drain beans and return to saucepan. Stir in 2½ cups
water, salt pork, onion, oregano, salt, ginger, sage and
pepper. Bring to a boil; reduce heat. Cover and simmer
2 to 2½ hours or until beans are tender. (If necessary,
add more water during cooking.) Add milk and butter,
stirring until mixture is heated through and butter is
melted. Season with additional salt and pepper, if
desired.   *Makes 6 servings*

Favorite recipe from **Wisconsin Milk Marketing Board**

Zucchini Chicken Soup

- ½ cup chopped onion
- ½ cup chopped carrot
- 1 clove garlic, minced
- 1 tablespoon butter or margarine
- 1 cup diced cooked chicken
- 1 can (14½ ounces) DEL MONTE® *FreshCut*™ Zucchini with Italian-Style Tomato Sauce
- 1 can (14½ ounces) chicken broth

Sauté onion, carrot and garlic in butter, about 5 minutes. Add remaining ingredients. Heat through and serve.
Makes 5 cups

Butch's Black Bean Soup

¼ cup olive oil
1 medium onion, diced
4 cloves garlic, minced
4 cups water
2 chicken-flavored bouillon cubes
1 large can (2 pounds, 8 ounces) black
    beans, drained and rinsed
2 cups canned corn (15 ounces),
    undrained
1 cup rice or orzo
3 celery stalks, diced
2 carrots, diced
1 medium potato, peeled and diced
¼ cup fresh cilantro, minced
2 (11-ounce) jars NEWMAN'S OWN®
    Bandito Salsa (medium or hot) *or*
    1 (26-ounce) jar NEWMAN'S OWN®
    Diavolo Sauce

Heat oil; cook and stir onion and garlic over high heat
until onion is translucent. Add water and bouillon
cubes; bring to a boil. Reduce heat to medium; add
beans, corn, rice, celery, carrots, potato and cilantro.
Stir in Newman's Own® Bandito Salsa and simmer
until rice and vegetables are cooked, about 30 minutes.

Makes 8 servings

Pea Soup

2 tablespoons butter or margarine
1 medium onion, chopped
1 bag (16 ounces) BIRDS EYE® frozen
 Green Peas
1 can (13¾ ounces) chicken broth
½ teaspoon dried tarragon

• Melt butter in medium saucepan over medium-high heat. Add onion; cook until tender, about 3 minutes.

• Add peas, chicken broth and tarragon. Bring to boil; reduce heat to medium. Cover and cook 4 minutes.

• Transfer mixture to blender; blend until smooth. Strain, if desired. Serve hot or cold.

Makes about 3 servings

Creamy Shell Soup

4 cups water
3 to 4 chicken pieces
1 cup diced onion
¼ cup chopped celery
¼ cup minced parsley *or* 1 tablespoon
   dried parsley flakes
1 bay leaf
1 teaspoon salt
¼ teaspoon white pepper
2 medium potatoes, diced
4 to 5 green onions, chopped
3 chicken bouillon cubes
½ teaspoon seasoned salt
½ teaspoon poultry seasoning
4 cups milk
2 cups medium shell macaroni, cooked
   and drained
¼ cup butter or margarine
¼ cup all-purpose flour
   Ground nutmeg
   Chopped fresh parsley

Simmer water, chicken, diced onion, celery, minced
parsley, bay leaf, salt and pepper in Dutch oven until
chicken is tender. Remove bay leaf; discard. Remove
chicken; cool. Skin, debone and cut chicken into small
cubes; set aside.

Add potatoes, green onions, bouillon cubes, seasoned salt and poultry seasoning to broth. Simmer 15 minutes. Add milk, macaroni and chicken; return to simmer.

Melt butter in skillet over medium heat. Add flour, stirring constantly, until mixture begins to brown. Add to soup; blend well.

Simmer on very low heat 20 minutes to blend flavors. Season to taste. Garnish with nutmeg and chopped parsley. *Makes 8 servings*

Favorite recipe from **North Dakota Wheat Commission**

Lentil Soup

1   tablespoon FILIPPO BERIO® Olive Oil
1   medium onion, diced
4   cups beef broth
1   cup dried lentils, rinsed and drained
¼   cup tomato sauce
1   teaspoon dried Italian herb seasoning
    Salt and freshly ground black pepper

In large saucepan, heat olive oil over medium heat
until hot. Add onion; cook and stir 5 minutes or until
softened. Add beef broth; bring mixture to a boil. Stir
in lentils, tomato sauce and Italian seasoning. Cover;
reduce heat to low and simmer 45 minutes or until
lentils are tender. Season to taste with salt and pepper.
Serve hot.   *Makes 6 servings*

Minestrone

3   slices (3 ounces) bacon, chopped
½   cup chopped onion
3½ cups (two 14½-ounce cans) beef broth
2   cups (15-ounce can) great Northern
        white beans, undrained
2   cups (1-pound 1-ounce can)
        CONTADINA® Dalla Casa Buitoni
        Country Italian Cooking Sauce with
        Garden Vegetables
2   cups (2 medium) sliced zucchini
2   cups (10-ounce package) frozen mixed
        vegetables
½   cup dried small macaroni
½   cup (2 ounces) grated Parmesan cheese

COMBINE bacon and onion in large saucepan. Cook
over medium-high heat for 4 to 5 minutes or until
bacon is crispy; drain. Stir in broth, beans and liquid
and cooking sauce; bring to a boil. Reduce heat to low;
cook for 5 minutes.

STIR in zucchini, mixed vegetables and macaroni;
bring to a boil. Reduce heat to low; cook for 8 to 10
minutes or until vegetables and pasta are tender.
Sprinkle with cheese.   *Makes 6 servings*

Hearty Tortilla Chip Soup

1   cup chopped onion
¾   cup finely chopped carrots
1   clove garlic, minced
6   ounces GUILTLESS GOURMET®
     Unsalted or Blue Corn Baked Tortilla
     Chips, divided
3   cans (14½ ounces *each*) low sodium
     chicken broth, defatted
2   cups water
½   cup each GUILTLESS GOURMET®
     Roasted Red Pepper and Green
     Tomatillo Salsas
1   can (6 ounces) low sodium tomato
     paste
1   cup (4 ounces) shredded low fat
     Monterey Jack cheese

Microwave Directions: Combine onion, carrots and
garlic in 3-quart microwave-safe casserole. Cover with
vented plastic wrap or lid; microwave on HIGH
(100% power) 7 minutes or until vegetables are tender.
Finely crush half the tortilla chips. Add crushed chips,
broth, water, salsas and tomato paste; stir well. Cover;
microwave on HIGH 6 minutes or until soup bubbles.
Microwave on MEDIUM (50% power) 5 minutes. To
serve, divide remaining tortilla chips and half the
cheese among 6 individual soup bowls. Ladle soup over
cheese and chips, dividing evenly. Sprinkle with
remaining cheese.   *Makes 8 servings*

Stove Top Directions: Bring 2 tablespoons broth
to a boil in 3-quart saucepan over medium-high heat.
Add onion, carrots and garlic; cook and stir about 5
minutes or until vegetables are tender. Finely crush
half the tortilla chips. Add crushed chips, remaining
broth, water, salsas and tomato paste; stir well. Cook
over medium heat until soup comes to a boil. Reduce
heat to low; simmer 5 minutes. Serve as directed.

Tortilla Rice Soup

Vegetable cooking spray
⅓ cup sliced green onions
4 cups chicken broth
2 cups cooked rice
1 can (10½ ounces) diced tomatoes with
    green chiles, undrained
1 cup cooked chicken breast cubes
1 can (4 ounces) chopped green chiles,
    undrained
1 tablespoon lime juice
    Salt to taste
    Tortilla chips
½ cup chopped tomato
½ avocado, cut into small cubes
4 lime slices, for garnish
    Fresh cilantro, for garnish

Heat Dutch oven or large saucepan coated with
cooking spray over medium-high heat until hot. Add
onions; cook and stir until tender. Add broth, rice,
tomatoes and juice, chicken and chiles. Reduce heat to
low; cover and simmer 20 minutes. Stir in lime juice
and salt. Just before serving, pour into soup bowls; top
with tortilla chips, tomato and avocado. Garnish with
lime slices and cilantro.   *Makes 4 servings*

Favorite recipe from **USA Rice Council**

Southwestern Soup

1 bag (16 ounces) BIRDS EYE® frozen
   Corn
½ cup chopped green bell pepper
2 cans (15 ounces each) chili
1 cup hot water

- Combine all ingredients in saucepan.

- Cook over medium heat 10 to 12 minutes.

Makes 4 to 6 servings

Hot & Sour Soup

1   **can (10½ ounces) condensed chicken
     broth**
2   **soup cans water**
1   **can (4 ounces) sliced mushrooms**
2   **tablespoons cornstarch**
2   **tablespoons KIKKOMAN® Soy Sauce**
2   **tablespoons distilled white vinegar**
½   **teaspoon TABASCO® pepper sauce**
1   **egg, beaten**
2   **green onions and tops, chopped**

Combine chicken broth, water, mushrooms,
cornstarch, soy sauce, vinegar and TABASCO® sauce in
medium saucepan. Bring to boil over high heat,
stirring constantly, until slightly thickened. Gradually
pour egg into boiling soup, stirring constantly in 1
direction. Remove from heat; stir in green onions.
Garnish with additional chopped green onions or
cilantro as desired. Serve immediately.

Makes 4 to 6 servings

Ginger Wonton Soup

- 4 ounces lean ground pork
- ½ cup reduced-fat ricotta cheese
- ½ tablespoon minced fresh cilantro
- ½ teaspoon ground black pepper
- ⅛ teaspoon Chinese 5-spice powder
- 20 fresh or frozen, thawed wonton skins
- 1 teaspoon vegetable oil
- ⅓ cup chopped red bell pepper
- 1 teaspoon grated fresh ginger
- 2 cans (14½ ounces *each*) fat-free reduced-sodium chicken broth
- 2 teaspoons reduced-sodium soy sauce
- 4 ounces fresh pea pods
- 1 can (8¾ ounces) baby corn, rinsed and drained
- 2 green onions, thinly sliced

Cook pork in small nonstick skillet over medium-high heat until no longer pink. Cool slightly; stir in ricotta cheese, cilantro, black pepper and 5-spice powder. Place 1 teaspoon filling in center of each wonton skin. Fold top corner of wonton over filling. Lightly brush remaining corners with water. Fold left and right corners over filling. Tightly roll filled end toward remaining corner in jelly-roll fashion. Moisten edges with water to seal. Cover and set aside.

Heat oil in large saucepan. Add bell pepper and ginger; cook 1 minute. Add chicken broth and soy sauce; bring to a boil. Add pea pods, baby corn and wontons. Reduce heat to medium-low; simmer 4 to 5 minutes or until wontons are tender. Sprinkle with onions.   *Makes 4 servings*

Onion Soup with Crouton Crust

ONION SOUP
- 1   tablespoon vegetable oil
- 3   pounds large yellow onions, halved and thinly sliced (about 9 cups)
- 3   tablespoons all-purpose flour
- ⅔   cup apple brandy or water
- 5   cups low sodium beef stock or broth
- 2⅓ cups low sodium chicken stock or broth
- 1   tablespoon snipped fresh thyme leaves *or* 1 teaspoon dried thyme
- 1   teaspoon freshly ground black pepper
- ¼   teaspoon salt

CROUTON CRUST
- 8   slices (½ inch thick) whole wheat or white French bread
- ¾   cup (3 ounces) shredded ALPINE LACE® Reduced Fat Swiss Cheese

1. To make the Onion Soup: Spray a 6-quart Dutch oven or stockpot with nonstick cooking spray. Add the oil and heat over medium-high heat.

2. Add the onions and cook, stirring occasionally, for about 10 minutes or until browned and caramelized. Stir in the flour, then the brandy. Bring to a boil.

3. Add both of the stocks, the thyme, pepper and salt. Return to a boil, then reduce the heat to low and simmer, uncovered, for 30 minutes.

4. While the soup simmers, make the Crouton Crust: Preheat the broiler. Place the bread slices on a baking sheet and broil until nicely browned on both sides. Remove the bread slices from the baking sheet and set aside.

5. Place 8 ovenproof soup bowls on the baking sheet. Ladle the soup into the bowls and top each with a crouton. Sprinkle crouton and soup with the cheese. Broil 6 inches from the heat for 1 to 2 minutes or until cheese is melted and bubbly.

Makes 8 first-course servings
(1 cup each)

Tomato French Onion Soup

  4 medium onions, chopped
  2 tablespoons butter or margarine
  1 can (14½ ounces) DEL MONTE®
     FreshCut™ Diced Tomatoes
  1 can (10½ ounces) condensed beef
     consommé
  ¼ cup dry sherry
  4 French bread slices, toasted
1½ cups (6 ounces) shredded Swiss cheese
  ¼ cup (1 ounce) grated Parmesan cheese

1. Cook onions in butter in large saucepan about 10 minutes. Add undrained tomatoes, reserved liquid, 2 cups water, consommé and sherry to saucepan. Bring to boil, skimming off foam.

2. Reduce heat to medium-low; simmer 10 minutes. Place soup in four broiler-proof bowls; top with bread and cheeses. Broil until cheeses are melted and golden.

Makes 4 servings

Tip: If broiler-proof bowls are not available, place soup in ovenproof bowls and bake at 350°F 10 minutes.

Garden Fresh Gazpacho

SOUP BASE
- 4 large tomatoes (about 2 pounds)
- 1 large cucumber, peeled and seeded
- ½ each red and green bell pepper, seeded
- ½ red onion
- 3 cloves garlic
- 2 tablespoons minced fresh basil
- ¼ cup FRANK'S® Original REDHOT® Cayenne Pepper Sauce
- ¼ cup red wine vinegar
- 3 tablespoons olive oil
- 1 teaspoon salt

GARNISH
- 2 cups chopped vegetables, such as tomatoes, bell peppers, cucumber and/or green onions

Coarsely chop Soup Base vegetables; place vegetables and remaining Soup Base ingredients in food processor or blender. Cover and process until smooth. (If necessary, process vegetables in batches.) Transfer soup to large glass bowl. Stir in chopped vegetables, leaving some to sprinkle on top for garnish, if desired. Cover and refrigerate 1 hour before serving. Divide among 6 individual serving bowls. Sprinkle with remaining garnish.   *Makes 6 (1-cup) servings*

Creamy Gazpacho

1¾ cups (14.5-ounce can) CONTADINA®
   Dalla Casa Buitoni Recipe Ready
   Diced Tomatoes, drained
2 cups (16 ounces) tomato juice
1 cup CARNATION® Evaporated
   Skimmed Milk
3 tablespoons lemon juice
2 tablespoons olive oil
1 clove garlic, finely chopped
½ teaspoon salt
¼ teaspoon ground black pepper
¼ teaspoon hot pepper sauce
2 cups (2 medium) peeled, seeded and
   chopped cucumbers
½ cup chopped green bell pepper
½ cup chopped onion
   Garnishes: plain low-fat or nonfat
      yogurt, chopped cucumber, bell
      pepper and onion

PLACE tomatoes, tomato juice, evaporated milk, lemon juice, oil, garlic, salt, pepper and hot pepper sauce in blender container; cover. Blend thoroughly (container will be very full).

POUR into pitcher or tureen. Add cucumbers, bell pepper and onion; stir thoroughly. Chill.

SERVE cold. Garnish as desired.

Makes 5 servings

Chilled Zucchini-Basil Soup

2   cups chicken broth
3   medium zucchini, sliced
2   medium onions, chopped
1   tablespoon minced fresh basil *or*
        1 teaspoon dried basil leaves, crushed
1   clove garlic, sliced
½   cup HELLMANN'S® or BEST FOODS®
        Real or Light Mayonnaise or Low Fat
        Mayonnaise Dressing
2   tablespoons lemon juice
⅛   teaspoon hot pepper sauce

1. In 3-quart saucepan, combine chicken broth, zucchini, onions, basil and garlic. Bring to a boil over high heat. Reduce heat to low; cover and simmer 10 minutes or until zucchini is tender. Cool.

2. In blender or food processor container, place zucchini mixture, half at a time. Process until smooth. Pour into large bowl. Stir in mayonnaise, lemon juice and hot pepper sauce until well blended.

3. Cover; refrigerate several hours or overnight.

Makes about 4 cups

Cool Italian Tomato Soup

2 cups (16 ounces) tomato juice
1¾ cups (14-ounce can) CONTADINA®
Dalla Casa Butioni Pasta Ready
Chunky Tomatoes with Spicy Red
Pepper, undrained
½ cup half-and-half
2 tablespoons lemon juice
2 cups (1 large) peeled chopped
cucumber
½ cup chopped green bell pepper
Fresh basil and croutons (optional)

COMBINE tomato juice, tomatoes and juice,
half-and-half and lemon juice in blender container;
cover. Process until smooth. Pour into large bowl. Stir
in cucumber and bell pepper. Top with basil and
croutons just before serving, if desired.

Makes 4 to 6 servings

Chilled Avocado Soup

1   tablespoon FILIPPO BERIO® Olive Oil
1   bunch green onions, trimmed and
     sliced
1   tablespoon all-purpose flour
2   cups chicken broth
2   large ripe avocados, halved, pitted and
     peeled
2   cups milk
½   cup plain low fat yogurt
2   teaspoons lemon juice
     Salt and white pepper

In large saucepan or Dutch oven, heat olive oil over
medium heat until hot. Add green onions; cook and
stir 2 minutes. Add flour; stir until mixture is smooth.
Cook 1 minute. Gradually whisk in chicken broth.
Cover; reduce heat to low and simmer 10 minutes.
Cool slightly. Meanwhile, coarsely chop avocados.

In blender container or food processor, combine
avocados and chicken broth mixture; process until
smooth. Transfer to large bowl. Add milk, yogurt and
lemon juice. Blend with wire whisk or electric mixer at
medium speed until smooth. Season to taste with salt
and pepper. Cover; refrigerate at least 2 hours before
serving. Serve cold.   *Makes 4 to 6 servings*

Minted Melon Soup

1 **cup water**
1 **tablespoon sugar**
1½ **cups fresh mint, including stems**
2 **fresh basil leaves**
1½ **cups diced cantaloupe**
4 **teaspoons fresh lemon juice, divided**
1½ **cups diced and seeded watermelon**
4 **mint sprigs, for garnish (optional)**

1. To prepare mint syrup, combine water and sugar in small saucepan; mix well. Bring to a boil over medium heat. Add mint and basil; simmer 10 minutes or until liquid is reduced by two-thirds. Remove from heat; cover and let stand at least 2 hours or until cool. Strain syrup; set aside.

2. Place cantaloupe in food processor or blender; process until smooth. Add 2 tablespoons mint syrup and 2 teaspoons lemon juice. Blend to mix well. Pour into airtight container. Cover and refrigerate until cold. Repeat procedure with watermelon, 2 teaspoons mint syrup and remaining 2 teaspoons lemon juice. Discard any remaining mint syrup.

3. To serve, simultaneously pour ¼ cup of each melon soup, side by side, into serving bowl. Place 1 mint sprig in center for garnish, if desired. Repeat with remaining soup.   *Makes 4 appetizer servings*

Refreshing Strawberry Soup

2 cups hulled strawberries, cold
1 cup low-fat buttermilk
4 teaspoons sugar

In food processor or blender container, process strawberries, buttermilk and sugar until smooth. Serve immediately or cover and refrigerate. Garnish as desired.   *Makes 4 servings*

Favorite recipe from **The Sugar Association, Inc.**

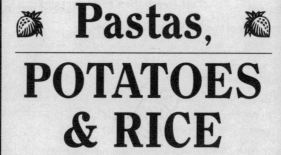

Pastas, POTATOES & RICE

Zesty Pasta Salad

3 ounces uncooked tricolor rotini pasta
1 cup sliced mushrooms
¾ cup pasta-ready canned tomatoes,
    undrained
½ cup sliced green bell pepper
¼ cup chopped onion
¼ cup fat-free Italian salad dressing
2 tablespoons grated Parmesan cheese
    Lettuce leaves, for garnish (optional)

1. Cook pasta according to package directions, omitting salt. Rinse with cool water; drain. Cool.

2. Combine pasta, mushrooms, tomatoes with liquid, pepper and onion in large bowl. Pour Italian dressing over pasta mixture; toss to coat.

3. Top with cheese before serving. Garnish with lettuce leaves, if desired.   *Makes 6 servings*

Rotini Salad

10 ounces uncooked rotini
2 to 3 stalks broccoli, chopped, cooked
     and drained
1 can (6 ounces) small pitted ripe olives,
     drained
10 to 12 cherry tomatoes, cut into halves
½ medium red onion, cut into slivers
½ cup Italian salad dressing
1 to 2 tablespoons grated Parmesan
     cheese (optional)
   Freshly ground black pepper

1. Cook pasta according to package directions. Drain in colander. Cover and refrigerate until chilled.

2. Combine pasta, broccoli, olives, tomatoes, onion and salad dressing in large bowl. Add cheese, if desired. Season to taste with pepper. Toss gently to coat.

3. Cover; refrigerate at least 2 hours.

Makes 8 to 10 servings

Favorite recipe from **North Dakota Wheat Commission**

Tortellini with Artichokes, Olives and Feta Cheese

2   **packages (9 ounces *each*) refrigerated cheese-filled spinach tortellini**
2   **jars (4 ounces *each*) marinated artichoke heart quarters, drained***
2   **medium carrots, sliced diagonally**
½   **cup sliced pitted ripe olives**
½   **cup (2 ounces) crumbled feta cheese**
½   **cup cheese-garlic Italian salad dressing**

1. Cook pasta according to package directions. Remove and rinse well under cold water until pasta is cool.

2. Combine pasta, artichoke hearts, carrots, olives and feta cheese in large bowl. Add salad dressing; toss lightly. Season to taste with pepper.

Makes 6 servings

*For additional flavor, add artichoke marinade to tortellini along with salad dressing.

Artichoke and Olive Pasta Salad

1 package (12 ounces) dried
    CONTADINA® Dalla Casa Buitoni
    Tricolor Rotelle pasta, cooked,
    drained
2 cups (1-pound 1-ounce can)
    CONTADINA® Dalla Casa Buitoni
    Country Italian Cooking Sauce with
    Garden Vegetables
¾ cup (6-ounce jar) marinated artichoke
    hearts, coarsely chopped, marinade
    reserved
½ cup prepared Italian salad dressing
½ cup (2¼-ounce can) sliced ripe olives,
    drained
¼ cup chopped fresh parsley
¼ cup sliced green onions (about 3)

COMBINE pasta, cooking sauce, artichoke hearts,
reserved marinade, salad dressing, olives, parsley and
green onions in large bowl; toss well. Chill for 1 hour.

Makes 8 to 10 servings

Santa Fe Pasta Salad

8 ounces medium shell pasta
   (3 cups uncooked)
1 can (15¼ ounces) red kidney beans,
   drained and rinsed
1 can (7 ounces) corn kernels, drained
1 green or red bell pepper, seeded and
   chopped
1 cup (4 ounces) shredded Cheddar
   cheese
½ cup sliced black olives
1 bottle (8 ounces) salsa ranch salad
   dressing
2 tablespoons FRANK'S® Original
   REDHOT® Cayenne Pepper Sauce
1 teaspoon chili powder
3 bell peppers (green, red and/or yellow),
   halved and seeded (optional)

Cook pasta according to package directions; rinse in
cold water and drain. Place in large bowl. Add beans,
corn, chopped pepper, cheese and olives. Combine
salad dressing, RedHot® sauce and chili powder in
small bowl; mix well. Pour over pasta mixture. Toss
well to coat evenly. Cover and refrigerate 1 hour. Serve
in pepper halves and garnish as desired.

Makes 6 side-dish servings

Pesto Pasta Salad

2   cups firmly packed washed fresh basil
       leaves
1   cup firmly packed washed fresh parsley
¼   cup slivered almonds
¼   cup (1 ounce) grated Parmesan cheese
3   cloves garlic, coarsely chopped
½   cup FRENCH'S® Dijon Mustard
1   tablespoon FRENCH'S® Worcestershire
       Sauce
⅔   cup olive oil
4   cups cooked small pasta
       (about ½ pound uncooked), drained
       and rinsed with cold water
     Chopped seeded red bell peppers or
       tomatoes

To prepare **Dijon Pesto Sauce,** place basil, parsley,
almonds, cheese and garlic in food processor. Cover
and process until finely chopped. Add mustard and
Worcestershire; process until well blended. Gradually
add oil in steady stream, processing until thick sauce
forms.

Place pasta in large bowl. Pour pesto sauce over pasta;
toss well to coat evenly. Cover and refrigerate until
ready to serve. Garnish with peppers.

Makes 6 side-dish servings
(about 2 cups sauce)

Pasta Primavera Salad

- ¾ pound corkscrew pasta, cooked and drained
- 3 tablespoons olive or vegetable oil
- 1 cup broccoli flowerets, steamed crisp-tender
- ½ cup cherry tomato halves
- ⅓ cup sliced radishes
- 1 large red or green bell pepper, cut into small chunks
- 2 medium zucchini, cut into ¼-inch slices
- 3 green onions, chopped
- 2 tablespoons capers (optional)
- 1 cup prepared HIDDEN VALLEY RANCH® Original Ranch® salad dressing

In large bowl, toss pasta with oil; cool. Add remaining ingredients and toss again. Cover and refrigerate at least 2 hours. Just before serving, add more salad dressing, if desired.   *Makes 4 servings*

Mediterranean Pasta Salad

2 ounces uncooked bow tie pasta
1 cup canned garbanzo beans
   (chick-peas), rinsed and drained
1 cup cooked canned artichoke hearts,
   rinsed, drained, quartered
¾ cup sliced zucchini, halved
¼ cup chopped red onion
3 tablespoons lemon juice
2 tablespoons olive oil
½ teaspoon Italian seasoning
⅛ teaspoon ground black pepper
⅛ teaspoon garlic powder
2 tablespoons crumbled feta cheese
   Lettuce leaves (optional)

1. Cook pasta according to package directions, omitting salt. Rinse with cool water; drain. Cool.

2. Combine pasta, beans, artichoke hearts, zucchini and onion in large bowl.

3. Combine lemon juice, oil, Italian seasoning, pepper and garlic powder in small bowl until well blended. Drizzle over pasta mixture; toss to coat. Top with cheese before serving. Serve on lettuce leaves, if desired.   *Makes 6 servings*

Greek Pesto Salad

1   package (7 ounces) DI GIORNO® Pesto
    Sauce
¼   cup red wine vinegar
1   package (9 ounces) DI GIORNO®
    Linguine, cooked, drained
1   medium red pepper, cut into 1-inch
    chunks
1   medium yellow pepper, cut into 1-inch
    chunks
1   cup chopped cucumber
¼   cup pitted chopped Greek olives
4   ounces ATHENOS® Feta Natural
    Cheese, crumbled

STIR sauce and vinegar in medium bowl. Toss in pasta until well coated.

TOSS peppers, cucumber and olives in medium bowl. Refrigerate.

PLACE pasta on serving platter or in large bowl. Top with vegetables. Sprinkle with cheese.

Makes 6 to 8 servings

Garden Vegetable Pasta Salad with Bacon

 12 ounces uncooked rotini or spiral pasta
 ½ pound bacon, thinly sliced
 1 medium bunch broccoli, cut into florets
 2 medium carrots, sliced diagonally
 2 ribs celery, sliced diagonally
 1 can (14½ ounces) pasta-ready tomatoes, drained
 10 medium mushrooms, thinly sliced
 ½ medium red or yellow onion, thinly sliced
 1 bottle (8 ounces) ranch salad dressing
 ½ cup (2 ounces) shredded Cheddar cheese
 1 tablespoon dried parsley flakes
 2 teaspoons dried basil leaves
 ¼ teaspoon black pepper

1. Cook pasta according to package directions. Drain and rinse well under cold water until pasta is cool.

2. Heat large skillet over medium-high heat. Add bacon; cook until browned. Remove bacon from skillet; drain on paper towels. Cool and crumble into small pieces.

3. Combine broccoli, carrots, celery, tomatoes, mushrooms and onion in large bowl. Add pasta and bacon; toss lightly. Add salad dressing, Cheddar cheese, parsley, basil and pepper; stir to combine.

Makes 6 servings

Curried Pasta Salad

4 ounces uncooked bow tie or corkscrew
   (fusilli) pasta
1 can (8 ounces) DOLE® Pineapple
   Chunks
½ cup fat free or reduced fat mayonnaise
2 teaspoons packed brown sugar
1 teaspoon curry powder
1 can (11 ounces) DOLE® Mandarin
   Oranges, drained
1½ cups cooked chicken breast or turkey
   breast strips
½ cup sliced DOLE® Celery
¼ cup chopped DOLE® Green Onions

• **Cook** pasta as package directs; drain.

• **Drain** pineapple; reserve 3 tablespoons juice.

• **Stir** reserved juice, mayonnaise, sugar and curry in large serving bowl until blended.

• **Add** pasta, pineapple, mandarin oranges, chicken, celery and green onions to curry dressing; toss to evenly coat. Serve on lettuce-lined plate and garnish with shredded red cabbage, if desired.

Makes 4 servings

Confetti Barley Salad

4 cups water
1 cup dry pearl barley
⅓ cup GREY POUPON® Dijon Mustard
⅓ cup olive oil
¼ cup REGINA® Red Wine Vinegar
2 tablespoons chopped parsley
2 teaspoons chopped fresh rosemary
leaves *or* ½ teaspoon dried rosemary
leaves
2 teaspoons grated orange peel
1 teaspoon sugar
1½ cups diced red, green or yellow bell
peppers
½ cup sliced green onions
½ cup sliced pitted ripe olives
Fresh rosemary and orange and tomato
slices, for garnish

In 3-quart saucepan, over medium-high heat, bring water and barley to a boil; reduce heat. Cover; simmer for 45 to 55 minutes or until tender. Drain and cool.

In small bowl, whisk mustard, oil, vinegar, parsley, rosemary, orange peel and sugar until blended; set aside.

In large bowl, combine barley, bell peppers, green onions and olives. Stir in mustard dressing, tossing to coat well. Chill several hours to blend flavors. To serve, spoon barley mixture onto serving platter; garnish with rosemary and orange and tomato slices.

Makes 6 to 8 servings

Singapore Rice Salad

1 can (8 ounces) pineapple tidbits or chunks in pineapple juice, undrained
3 cups chilled cooked white rice, prepared in salted water
1 cup diced cucumber
1 red bell pepper, diced
1 cup shredded carrots
½ cup sliced green onions
2 tablespoons fresh lime juice
2 tablespoons dry sherry
1 tablespoon rice wine vinegar
1 teaspoon minced fresh ginger
2 tablespoons chopped fresh cilantro
1 tablespoon chopped unsalted peanuts
  Cucumber slices, for garnish

Drain pineapple, reserving 3 tablespoons juice. Set juice aside. In large bowl combine pineapple, rice, cucumber, bell pepper, carrots and onions.

In small bowl combine lime juice, sherry, vinegar, ginger and reserved pineapple juice; mix well. Pour over rice mixture; toss to coat. Cover and refrigerate at least 2 hours. Sprinkle with cilantro and peanuts before serving. Garnish with cucumber slices.

Makes 6 side-dish servings

Florida Rice and Avocado Salad

- 3 cups cooked rice, cooled
- 2 cups chopped cooked chicken
- 2 avocados, peeled and cut into ½-inch cubes
- 1 cup diagonally sliced celery
- ½ green bell pepper, cut into julienned strips
- ¼ cup minced onion
- 3 tablespoons lemon juice
- 2 tablespoons vegetable oil
- 1½ teaspoons salt
- 1 teaspoon sugar
- ¼ teaspoon ground white pepper
- 1 clove garlic, minced
  Hot pepper sauce to taste
  Salad greens (optional)
  Tomato wedges or roses, for garnish

Combine rice, chicken, avocados, celery, green pepper and onion in large bowl. Place lemon juice, oil, salt, sugar, white pepper, garlic and pepper sauce in small jar with lid; shake well. Pour over rice mixture. Toss lightly. Cover and refrigerate 1 to 2 hours. Adjust seasonings, if necessary. Serve over salad greens, if desired. Garnish with tomato wedges.

Makes 6 servings

Favorite recipe from **USA Rice Council**

Confetti Wild Rice Salad

1   **package (6 ounces) white and wild rice mix**
1   **each red and yellow bell pepper, seeded and chopped**
¼   **cup finely chopped red onion**
¼   **cup minced fresh parsley**
¼   **cup minced fresh basil leaves**
⅓   **cup FRENCH'S® Dijon Mustard**
¼   **cup olive oil**
¼   **cup red wine vinegar**

Prepare rice according to package directions; cool completely. Place rice in large bowl. Add peppers, onion, parsley and basil. Combine mustard, oil and vinegar in small bowl; mix well. Pour over rice and vegetables; toss well to coat evenly. Cover and refrigerate 1 hour before serving. Garnish as desired.

Makes 8 side-dish servings

Mediterranean Vegetable Salad

2   cups instant couscous
8   cups coarsely chopped vegetables, such
      as cucumbers, tomatoes, radishes,
      celery, green bell peppers and/or red
      onions
1   cup olive oil
¼   cup FRENCH'S® Dijon Mustard
¼   cup lemon juice
2   tablespoons minced fresh basil leaves
      or 2 teaspoons dried basil leaves
2   teaspoons minced fresh thyme leaves *or*
      1 teaspoon dried thyme leaves
2   cloves garlic, minced
1   teaspoon salt
4   ounces goat cheese, crumbled

Prepare couscous according to package directions; fluff
with fork. Spread couscous on large serving platter.

Place vegetables in large bowl. Place oil, mustard,
lemon juice, herbs, garlic and salt in blender or food
processor. Cover and process until well blended. Pour
dressing over vegetables; toss well to coat evenly. To
serve, arrange vegetables over couscous; sprinkle with
cheese.   *Makes 8 side-dish servings*

Dijon Asparagus Chicken Salad

1 cup HELLMANN'S® or BEST FOODS®
    Real or Light Mayonnaise or Low Fat
    Mayonnaise Dressing
¼ cup HELLMANN'S® or BEST FOODS®
    DIJONNAISE Creamy Mustard Blend
2 tablespoons lemon juice
1 teaspoon salt
½ teaspoon black pepper
1 pound boneless skinless chicken
    breasts, cooked and cubed
1 package (10 ounces) frozen asparagus
    spears, thawed and cut into 2-inch
    pieces
6 ounces MUELLER'S® Twist Trio®,
    cooked, rinsed with cold water and
    drained
1 red bell pepper, cut into 1-inch squares

1. In large bowl, stir mayonnaise, creamy mustard blend, lemon juice, salt and black pepper.

2. Add chicken, asparagus, pasta and red bell pepper; toss to coat well.

3. Cover; chill to blend flavors.   *Makes 6 servings*

Classic Potato Salad

1 cup HELLMANN'S® or BEST FOODS®
   Real or Light Mayonnaise or Low Fat
   Mayonnaise Dressing
2 tablespoons vinegar
1½ teaspoons salt
1 teaspoon sugar
¼ teaspoon freshly ground black pepper
5 to 6 medium potatoes, peeled, cubed
   and cooked
1 cup sliced celery
½ cup chopped onion
2 hard-cooked eggs, diced

1. In large bowl combine mayonnaise, vinegar, salt, sugar and pepper.

2. Add potatoes, celery, onion and eggs; toss to coat well.

3. Cover; chill to blend flavors.

Makes about 8 servings

Santa Fe Potato Salad

5   medium white potatoes
½   cup vegetable oil
¼   cup red wine vinegar
1   package (1.0 ounce) LAWRY'S® Taco
     Spices & Seasonings
1   can (7 ounces) whole kernel corn,
     drained
⅔   cup sliced celery
⅔   cup shredded carrot
⅔   cup chopped red or green bell pepper
2   cans (2.25 ounces each) sliced ripe
     olives, drained
½   cup chopped red onion
2   tomatoes, wedged and halved

In large saucepan, cook potatoes in boiling water until
tender, about 30 minutes; drain. Let cool slightly; cut
into cubes. In small bowl, combine oil, vinegar and
Taco Spices & Seasonings; blend well. Add to warm
potatoes; toss gently to coat. Cover; refrigerate at least
1 hour. Gently fold in remaining ingredients. Chill
thoroughly.   *Makes 8 servings*

Variation: Prepare potatoes as above. Replace vinegar
and oil with ½ cup *each* mayonnaise, sour cream and
salsa. Mix with Taco Spices & Seasonings and continue
as directed above.

Ranch Picnic Potato Salad

FAMILY SIZE RECIPE
  6 medium potatoes (about 3½ pounds),
       cooked, peeled and sliced
  ½ cup chopped celery
  ¼ cup sliced green onions
  2 tablespoons chopped parsley
  1 teaspoon salt
  ⅛ teaspoon black pepper
  1 tablespoon Dijon mustard
  1 cup prepared HIDDEN VALLEY
       RANCH® Original Ranch® salad
       dressing
  2 hard-cooked eggs, finely chopped
       Paprika

CROWD SIZE RECIPE
  6 pounds potatoes, cooked, peeled and
       sliced
  2 cups chopped celery
  1 cup sliced green onions
  ½ cup chopped parsley
  1 teaspoon salt
  1 teaspoon black pepper
  ¼ cup Dijon mustard
  1 quart prepared HIDDEN VALLEY
       RANCH® Original Ranch® salad
       dressing
  8 hard-cooked eggs, finely chopped
       Paprika

In large bowl, combine potatoes, celery, onions, parsley, salt and pepper. In small bowl, stir mustard into salad dressing; pour over potatoes and toss lightly. Cover and refrigerate several hours. Sprinkle with eggs and paprika. Serve in lettuce-lined bowl, if desired.

Family Size Recipe makes 8 servings
Crowd Size Recipe makes 25 servings

Country Bacon Potato Salad

2 pounds red potatoes, cooked, peeled and diced
⅓ cup chopped green, red or yellow bell pepper
1 small red onion, thinly sliced
6 slices bacon, cooked and crumbled
⅓ cup mayonnaise*
⅓ cup GREY POUPON® Dijon Mustard
2 tablespoons REGINA® Red Wine Vinegar
2 tablespoons chopped parsley
½ teaspoon garlic powder
½ teaspoon dried oregano leaves

In large bowl, combine potatoes, bell pepper, onion and bacon; set aside. In small bowl, blend remaining ingredients. Stir into potato mixture, tossing to coat well. Cover; chill at least 2 hours to blend flavors.

Makes 5 servings

*Low-fat mayonnaise may be substituted for regular mayonnaise.

Gourmet Deli Potato & Pea Salad

1½ pounds new potatoes, scrubbed and
   quartered
1 cup water
¾ teaspoon salt, divided
½ pound sugar snap peas or snow peas,
   trimmed
⅓ cup reduced fat mayonnaise
⅓ cup plain nonfat yogurt
3 tablespoons FRENCH'S® Dijon Mustard
⅓ cup finely chopped red onion
2 tablespoons minced fresh dill *or*
   2 teaspoons dried dill weed
1 clove garlic, minced

Place potatoes, water and ½ *teaspoon* salt in 3-quart
microwave-safe baking dish. Cover and microwave on
HIGH (100% power) 15 minutes or until potatoes are
tender, stirring once. Add peas. Cover and microwave
on HIGH 3 minutes or until peas are crisp-tender.
Rinse with cold water and drain. Cool completely.
Combine mayonnaise, yogurt, mustard, onion, dill,
garlic and remaining ¼ *teaspoon* salt in large bowl; mix
well. Add potatoes and peas; toss to coat evenly. Cover
and refrigerate 1 hour before serving. Garnish as
desired.   *Makes 6 side-dish servings*

Green Bean, New Potato & Ham Salad

    3 pounds new potatoes, quartered
    ⅔ cup cold water
    1 pound green beans, cut in half
    ¾ cup MIRACLE WHIP® FREE® Nonfat
       Dressing
    ⅓ cup stone ground mustard
    2 tablespoons red wine vinegar
    2 cups cubed OSCAR MAYER® Ham
    ½ cup chopped green onions

PLACE potatoes and water in 3-quart microwave-safe casserole; cover.

MICROWAVE on HIGH 13 minutes. Stir in beans. Microwave 7 to 13 minutes or until tender; drain.

MIX salad dressing, mustard and vinegar in large bowl until well blended. Add potatoes, beans and remaining ingredients; mix lightly. Refrigerate.

Makes 12 cups

Versatile

VEGGIES

Spinach, Bacon and Mushroom Salad

- 1 large bunch (12 ounces) fresh spinach leaves, washed, drained and torn
- ¾ cup sliced fresh mushrooms
- 4 slices bacon, cooked and crumbled
- ¾ cup croutons
- 4 hard-cooked eggs, finely chopped
  Black pepper to taste
- ¾ cup prepared HIDDEN VALLEY RANCH® Original Ranch® salad dressing

In medium salad bowl, combine spinach, mushrooms and bacon; toss. Top with croutons and eggs; season with pepper. Pour salad dressing over all.

Makes 6 servings

Warm Mushroom Salad

2 quarts mixed salad greens (such as spinach, arugula, curly endive and romaine)
3 tablespoons FILIPPO BERIO® Olive Oil
1 (10-ounce) package mushrooms, cleaned and quartered or sliced
3 shallots, chopped
1 clove garlic, crushed
2 tablespoons chopped fresh chives
2 tablespoons lemon juice
2 tablespoons balsamic vinegar
1 teaspoon sugar
1½ cups purchased garlic croutons
    Shavings of Parmesan cheese
    Salt and freshly ground black pepper

Tear salad greens into bite-size pieces. Arrange on 4 serving plates. In medium skillet, heat olive oil over medium heat until hot. Add mushrooms, shallots and garlic; cook and stir 3 to 5 minutes or until mushrooms are tender. Stir in chives, lemon juice, vinegar and sugar; simmer 30 seconds. Spoon mixture over salad greens. Top with croutons and Parmesan cheese. Season to taste with salt and pepper.

Makes 4 to 6 servings

Asian Slaw

½ small head napa cabbage, shredded
   (about 4 cups)*
3 carrots, shredded
2 red or yellow bell peppers, seeded and
   cut into very thin strips
¼ pound snow peas, trimmed and cut into
   thin strips
⅓ cup peanut oil
¼ cup rice vinegar
3 tablespoons FRENCH'S®
   Worcestershire Sauce
1 tablespoon Oriental sesame oil
1 tablespoon honey
2 cloves garlic, minced

Place vegetables in large bowl. Whisk peanut oil,
vinegar, Worcestershire, sesame oil, honey and garlic
in small bowl until well blended. Pour dressing over
vegetables; toss well to coat evenly. Cover and
refrigerate 1 hour before serving.

Makes 6 side-dish servings

*You may substitute 4 cups shredded green cabbage for napa
cabbage.

Greek Salad

8   leaves romaine lettuce
2   tomatoes, cut into eighths
1   medium red onion, sliced or 3 green
     onions, chopped
½   cucumber, sliced
2   ounces feta cheese, crumbled
3   tablespoons chopped fresh parsley
8   oil-cured black olives
4   anchovies (optional)
    French Salad Dressing (page 78)

Slice lettuce with knife into ⅛-inch-wide strips. In medium bowl, combine lettuce, tomatoes, onion, cucumber, cheese, parsley, olives and anchovies, if desired. Serve with French Salad Dressing.

Makes 4 to 6 servings

Creamy Dijon Coleslaw

½ cup GREY POUPON® COUNTRY
 DIJON® Mustard
½ cup prepared ranch, creamy Italian or
 blue cheese salad dressing
2 tablespoons chopped parsley
½ teaspoon celery seed
3 cups shredded green cabbage
2 cups shredded red cabbage
1 cup shredded carrots
½ cup chopped onion
⅓ cup chopped red bell pepper

In small bowl, blend mustard, salad dressing, parsley
and celery seed; set aside.

In large bowl, combine green and red cabbages,
carrots, onion and bell pepper. Add mustard mixture,
tossing to coat well. Chill at least 1 hour before
serving.   *Makes about 5 cups*

Marinated Green Bean and Potato Salad

- 1 pound fresh green beans, washed and trimmed
- 4 cups cubed red potatoes
- ¼ cup red wine vinegar
- 2 tablespoons olive oil
- 2 tablespoons fresh lemon juice
- 4 cloves garlic, crushed
- 2 teaspoons honey
- 1 teaspoon salt
- 1 teaspoon dried dill weed
- 1 teaspoon dried thyme leaves
- ½ teaspoon black pepper
- 4 cups ready-to-use fresh spinach, torn into bite-sized pieces
- 1 medium tomato, cut into wedges, for garnish

1. Bring 4 quarts water to a boil in Dutch oven. Add green beans; reduce heat to medium and cook, covered, 8 minutes or until beans are crisp-tender. Remove beans with slotted spoon.

2. Add potatoes to same Dutch oven. Cook, covered, 12 to 15 minutes or until potatoes are tender. Remove potatoes; drain.

3. Combine vinegar, oil, lemon juice, garlic, honey, salt, dill weed, thyme and pepper in medium bowl; whisk to combine. Add green beans and potatoes; stir to combine. Cover and refrigerate up to 2 days, stirring occasionally.

4. Arrange spinach on serving platter. Spoon green bean mixture over spinach. Pour remaining marinade over top. Garnish with tomato wedges.

Makes 6 servings

Three-Bean Salad

1 (15½-ounce) can red kidney beans
1 (14½-ounce) can cut green beans
1 (14½-ounce) can yellow wax beans
1 green bell pepper, seeded and chopped
1 medium onion, chopped
2 ribs celery, sliced
¾ cup cider vinegar
⅓ cup FILIPPO BERIO® Olive Oil
2 tablespoons sugar
  Salt and freshly ground black pepper

Rinse and drain kidney beans. Drain green and wax beans. In large bowl, combine beans, bell pepper, onion and celery. In small bowl, whisk together vinegar, olive oil and sugar. Pour over bean mixture; toss until lightly coated. Cover; refrigerate several hours or overnight before serving. Season to taste with salt and black pepper. Store salad, covered, in refrigerator up to 1 week.   *Makes 10 to 12 servings*

Southwestern Bean and Corn Salad

1 can (about 15 ounces) pinto beans,
   rinsed and drained
1 cup fresh (about 2 ears) or thawed
   frozen corn
1 red bell pepper, finely chopped
4 green onions, finely chopped
2 tablespoons cider vinegar
2 tablespoons honey
½ teaspoon salt
½ teaspoon ground mustard
½ teaspoon ground cumin
1/8 teaspoon cayenne pepper
   Lettuce leaves (optional)

Combine beans, corn, bell pepper and onions in large bowl.

Blend vinegar and honey in small bowl until smooth. Stir in salt, mustard, cumin and cayenne pepper. Drizzle over bean mixture; toss to coat. Cover; refrigerate 2 hours. Serve on lettuce leaves, if desired.

Makes 4 servings

Roasted Red Pepper, Corn & Garbanzo Bean Salad

2   cans (15 ounces *each*) garbanzo beans
1   jar (11.5 ounces) GUILTLESS GOURMET® Roasted Red Pepper Salsa
1   cup frozen whole kernel corn, thawed and drained
½   cup GUILTLESS GOURMET® Green Tomatillo Salsa
2   green onions, thinly sliced
8   lettuce leaves
    Fresh tomato wedges and sunflower sprouts (optional)

Rinse and drain beans well; place in 2-quart casserole dish. Add roasted red pepper salsa, corn, tomatillo salsa and onions; stir to combine. Cover and refrigerate 1 hour or up to 24 hours.

To serve, line serving platter with lettuce. Spoon bean mixture over top. Garnish with tomatoes and sprouts, if desired.   *Makes 8 servings*

Zesty Zucchini Chick-Pea Salad

    3   medium zucchini
    ½   teaspoon salt
    5   tablespoons white vinegar
    1   clove garlic, minced
    ¼   teaspoon dried thyme leaves, crumbled
    ½   cup olive oil
    1   cup canned chick-peas, drained
    ½   cup sliced pitted ripe olives
    3   green onions, minced
    1   canned chipotle chili pepper in adobo
            sauce, drained, seeded and minced
    1   ripe avocado
    ⅓   cup crumbled feta *or* 3 tablespoons
            grated Romano cheese
        Boston lettuce leaves
        Sliced tomatoes and cilantro sprigs, for
            garnish (optional)

Cut zucchini lengthwise into halves; cut halves
crosswise into ¼-inch-thick slices. Place slices in
medium bowl; sprinkle with salt. Toss to mix. Spread
zucchini on several layers of paper towels. Let stand at
room temperature 30 minutes to drain.

Combine vinegar, garlic and thyme in large bowl.
Gradually add oil in thin, steady stream, whisking
continuously until dressing is thoroughly blended.

Pat zucchini dry; add to dressing. Add chick-peas,
olives and onions; toss lightly to coat. Cover;
refrigerate at least 30 minutes or up to 4 hours,
stirring occasionally.

Add chili pepper to salad just before serving. Stir gently to mix. Peel, pit and cut avocado into ½-inch cubes. Add avocado and cheese; toss lightly to mix.

Serve salad in lettuce-lined bowl or plate. Garnish, if desired.   *Makes 4 to 6 servings*

French Lentil Salad

1½   **cups lentils, rinsed, sorted and drained***
  4   **green onions, finely chopped**
  3   **tablespoons balsamic vinegar**
  2   **tablespoons chopped fresh parsley**
  1   **tablespoon olive oil**
  ¾   **teaspoon salt**
  ½   **teaspoon dried thyme leaves**
  ¼   **teaspoon ground black pepper**
1/4   **cup chopped walnuts, toasted**
      Lettuce leaves (optional)

Combine 2 quarts water and lentils in large saucepan; bring to a boil. Cover; reduce heat to medium-low. Simmer 30 minutes or until lentils are tender, stirring occasionally. Drain; discard liquid.

Combine lentils, onions, vinegar, parsley, oil, salt, thyme and pepper in large bowl. Cover; refrigerate at least 1 hour before serving. Serve on lettuce leaves, if desired. Top with walnuts just before serving. Garnish as desired.   *Makes 4 servings*

*Packages may contain grit and tiny stones. Thoroughly rinse. Then sort through and discard grit or any unusual looking pieces.

Wild Rice and Vegetable Salad

1 package (6.25 ounces) quick-cooking
 long grain and wild rice mix
1 bag (16 ounces) BIRDS EYE® frozen
 Farm Fresh Mixtures Cauliflower,
 Carrots and Snow Pea Pods
⅓ cup honey Dijon or favorite salad
 dressing
2 green onions, thinly sliced
¼ cup sliced almonds

• Cook rice according to package directions. Transfer to large bowl.

• Cook vegetables according to package directions. Drain; add to rice.

• Stir in dressing, green onions and almonds. Serve warm or cover and chill until ready to serve.

Makes about 4 side-dish servings

Market Salad

- 2 cups small cauliflower florets
- 2 cups small broccoli florets
- 2 cups (8 ounces) SARGENTO® Fancy Shredded Mozzarella Cheese
- 2 medium carrots, cut into short, thin strips
- 1 can (16 ounces) garbanzo beans, well drained
- ¾ cup chopped red bell pepper
- ⅓ cup white wine vinegar
- 2 cloves garlic, minced
- 1 teaspoon oregano, crushed
- ¼ teaspoon salt
- ½ cup vegetable oil
- 2 teaspoons capers (optional)

In large bowl, combine cauliflower, broccoli, Mozzarella cheese, carrots, beans and bell pepper; set aside. In small bowl, combine vinegar, garlic, oregano and salt. Slowly add oil, whisking until smooth and thickened. Stir in capers, if desired. Add to vegetable and cheese mixture. Toss gently. Cover; chill thoroughly, stirring several times.

Makes 8 servings

Tomato & Mozzarella Salad with Sun-Dried Tomato Dressing

DRESSING
- ⅓ cup water
- ¼ cup FRENCH'S® Worcestershire Sauce
- ¼ cup balsamic vinegar
- ¼ cup sun-dried tomatoes packed in oil, drained
- 2 tablespoons FRENCH'S® Dijon Mustard
- 2 cloves garlic, minced
- ½ cup olive oil

SALAD
- 6 cups washed and torn mixed salad greens
- 2 large ripe tomatoes, sliced
- 8 ounces fresh mozzarella cheese,* sliced
- 1 bunch asparagus, trimmed and blanched**
- 1 tablespoon minced fresh basil leaves

Place water, Worcestershire, vinegar, sun-dried tomatoes, mustard and garlic in blender or food processor. Cover and process until well blended. Gradually add oil in steady stream, processing until smooth. Set aside.

Place salad greens on large platter. Arrange tomatoes, cheese and asparagus on top. Sprinkle with basil. Serve with Dressing.   *Makes 6 to 8 side-dish servings*

*Look for fresh mozzarella in the deli section of your supermarket.

**To blanch asparagus, cook asparagus in boiling water 2 minutes. Drain and rinse with cold water.

Spinach Tomato Salad

1 package (8 ounces) DOLE® Complete
   Spinach Bacon Salad
2 medium tomatoes, halved and cut into
   thin wedges
½ medium cucumber, thinly sliced
½ small onion, thinly sliced
1 can (14 to 16 ounces) low-sodium
   kidney or garbanzo beans, drained

• **Toss** spinach, croutons and bacon from salad bag
with tomatoes, cucumber, onion and beans in medium
serving bowl.

• **Pour** dressing from packet over salad; toss to coat
evenly.   *Makes 4 servings*

Marinated Tomatoes & Mozzarella

1   **medium bunch fresh basil leaves, divided**
1   **pound Italian tomatoes, sliced**
½   **pound fresh packed buffalo mozzarella cheese, sliced**
¼   **cup olive oil**
3   **tablespoons chopped fresh chives**
2   **tablespoons red wine vinegar**
2   **teaspoons sugar**
½   **teaspoon dried oregano**
½   **teaspoon LAWRY'S® Seasoned Pepper**
½   **teaspoon LAWRY'S® Garlic Powder with Parsley**

Divide basil in half; reserve one half for garnish. Chop remaining basil leaves; set aside. In shallow dish, place tomato slices and cheese. Combine oil, chives, vinegar, sugar, oregano, Seasoned Pepper and Garlic Powder with Parsley in small bowl; pour over tomatoes and cheese. Cover. Refrigerate at least 30 minutes. To serve, arrange tomato and cheese slices on serving plate. Sprinkle with chopped basil leaves. Garnish with reserved whole basil leaves.

Makes 4 to 6 servings

Mixed Salad with Raspberry Honey Dijon Dressing

⅓ cup GREY POUPON® COUNTRY DIJON® Mustard*
⅓ cup dairy sour cream**
¼ cup raspberry-flavored vinegar
2 tablespoons honey*
4 cups mixed salad greens
1 cup cut green beans, steamed
1 cup cooked sliced beets
½ cup sliced mushrooms
½ cup shredded carrots
8 ounces turkey, cut into julienne strips

In small bowl, combine mustard, sour cream, vinegar and honey; chill dressing until serving time.

On large serving platter lined with salad greens, arrange vegetables and turkey. Drizzle with prepared dressing just before serving.   *Makes 6 servings*

*⅓ cup GREY POUPON® Honey Mustard may be substituted for COUNTRY DIJON® Mustard; omit honey.

**Low-fat sour cream may be substituted for regular sour cream.

Main

COURSE
SALADS

Turkey Curry Salad

DRESSING
- ½ cup nonfat mayonnaise
- ¼ cup plus 2 tablespoons skim milk
- 3 tablespoons lemon juice
- 1½ teaspoons curry powder
- ¾ teaspoon sugar
- ½ teaspoon salt

SALAD
- 1 pound DELI TURKEY BREAST, cut into ½-inch cubes
- 3 cups cooked long grain rice
- ½ jar (15 ounces) spiced red apples, chopped
- ½ cup slivered almonds, toasted
- 3 tablespoons finely chopped onion
  Leaf lettuce

In small bowl combine mayonnaise, milk, juice, curry powder, sugar and salt; set aside.

In large bowl combine turkey, rice, apples, almonds and onion. Fold in dressing. Cover and refrigerate until ready to serve.

To serve, arrange lettuce leaves on 6 salad plates and top each with heaping cup of salad.

Makes 6 servings

Favorite recipe from **National Turkey Federation**

Turkey & Pasta Waldorf Salad

½ **pound medium shell or tricolor rotini pasta, uncooked**
¾ **cup regular or reduced fat mayonnaise**
½ **cup FRENCH'S® Deli Brown Mustard**
⅓ **cup milk**
2 **tablespoons cider vinegar**
4 **teaspoons brown sugar**
½ **pound cubed low-salt deli turkey breast**
2 **ribs celery, chopped**
1 **apple, cored and chopped**
½ **cup halved green or red seedless grapes**
½ **cup chopped walnuts**

Cook pasta according to package directions. Drain and rinse with cold water. Drain thoroughly.

Combine mayonnaise, mustard, milk, vinegar and sugar in large bowl; mix well. Add pasta, turkey, celery, apple, grapes and nuts; toss well to coat evenly. Cover and refrigerate 1 hour before serving.

Makes 4 main-dish servings

Thai Beef Salad

DRESSING

- 1 cup olive oil vinaigrette salad dressing
- ⅓ cup FRANK'S® Original REDHOT® Cayenne Pepper Sauce
- 3 tablespoons chopped peeled fresh ginger
- 3 tablespoons sugar
- 3 cloves garlic, chopped
- 2 teaspoons FRENCH'S® Worcestershire Sauce
- 1 cup packed fresh mint or basil leaves, coarsely chopped

SALAD

- 1 flank steak (about 1½ pounds)
- 6 cups washed and torn mixed salad greens
- 1 cup sliced peeled cucumber
- ⅓ cup chopped peanuts

Place Dressing ingredients in blender or food processor. Cover; process until smooth. Reserve 1 cup Dressing. Place steak in large resealable plastic food storage bag. Pour remaining Dressing over steak. Seal bag and marinate in refrigerator 30 minutes. Place steak on grid, reserving marinade. Grill over high heat about 15 minutes for medium-rare, basting frequently with marinade. Let steak stand 5 minutes. To serve, slice steak diagonally and arrange on top of salad greens and cucumber. Sprinkle with nuts and drizzle with reserved 1 cup Dressing. Serve warm. Garnish as desired.   *Makes 6 servings*

Grilled Chicken Caesar Salad

½ **cup olive oil**
¼ **cup GREY POUPON® COUNTRY DIJON® Mustard**
2 **tablespoons lemon juice**
2 **teaspoons Worcestershire sauce**
1 **teaspoon grated lemon peel**
1 **clove garlic, minced**
½ **teaspoon sugar**
¼ **teaspoon coarsely ground black pepper**
1 **pound boneless skinless chicken breasts**
5 **cups torn romaine lettuce**
1 **cup sliced mushrooms**
1 **cup cherry tomato halves**
½ **cup prepared seasoned croutons**
1 **tablespoon grated Parmesan cheese**

In small bowl, whisk together oil, mustard, lemon juice, Worcestershire sauce, lemon peel, garlic, sugar and pepper. In nonmetal bowl, pour ¼ cup mustard dressing over chicken breasts, turning to coat. Cover and chill at least 1 hour. Chill remaining dressing until serving time.

Remove chicken from marinade; discard marinade. Grill or broil chicken breasts for 10 to 15 minutes or until done, turning once. Diagonally slice chicken breasts into strips.

In large bowl, combine lettuce, chicken, mushrooms, tomatoes and croutons. Toss with reserved dressing; sprinkle with Parmesan cheese and serve.

Makes 6 servings

Blue Cheese Chicken Salad

1 can (14½ ounces) DEL MONTE®
   FreshCut™ Diced Tomatoes with
   Garlic & Onion
½ pound boneless chicken breasts,
   skinned and cut into strips
½ teaspoon dried tarragon
6 cups torn assorted lettuces
½ medium red onion, thinly sliced
½ medium cucumber, thinly sliced
⅓ cup crumbled blue cheese
¼ cup Italian dressing

1. Drain tomatoes, reserving liquid. In large skillet, cook reserved liquid until thickened, about 5 minutes, stirring occasionally.

2. Add chicken and tarragon; cook until chicken is no longer pink, stirring frequently. Cool.

3. In large bowl, toss chicken and tomato liquid with remaining ingredients. *Makes 4 servings*

Golden Gate Chinese Chicken and Cabbage Sesame Salad

1½ pounds boneless skinless chicken
      breasts
1½ teaspoons salt-free lemon pepper
¼   teaspoon salt
8   cups thinly sliced napa cabbage
1   medium-size red bell pepper, cut into
      julienned strips
1   medium-size yellow bell pepper, cut
      into julienned strips
½   cup diagonally sliced green onions
½   cup sesame seeds, toasted
½   cup chopped dried apricots
3½ teaspoons grated fresh ginger, divided
¼   cup low-sodium chicken broth
¼   cup seasoned rice vinegar
¼   cup low-sodium soy sauce
2   tablespoons sugar
2   tablespoons dark sesame oil
6   napa cabbage leaves
1½ cups chow mein noodles

Place chicken in microwave-proof dish; sprinkle with
lemon pepper and salt. Cover with waxed paper and
microwave on HIGH (100%) 8 to 10 minutes or until
no longer pink in centers, rotating dish half turn every

2 minutes. Remove chicken from dish. Cool; discard liquid. Shred chicken into bite-size pieces. Combine chicken, sliced cabbage, red pepper, yellow pepper, onions, sesame seeds, apricots and 1 tablespoon ginger in large bowl. Toss well; cover and refrigerate until ready to serve. Combine broth, vinegar, soy sauce, sugar, oil and remaining ½ teaspoon ginger in small jar with lid; shake well. Pour over chicken and cabbage mixture; toss gently. Spoon onto individual plates lined with cabbage leaves. Sprinkle evenly with chow mein noodles. Serve immediately.   *Makes 6 servings*

Favorite recipe from **National Broiler Council**

Border Black Bean Chicken Salad

- ¼ cup olive oil, divided
- 1½ pounds boneless skinless chicken breasts, cut into 2-inch strips
- 1 clove garlic, minced
- ½ jalapeño pepper, seeded and finely chopped
- 1¼ teaspoons salt, divided
- 4 cups torn romaine lettuce
- 1 can (15 to 16 ounces) black beans, drained and rinsed
- 1 cup peeled, seeded, chopped cucumber
- 1 cup red bell pepper strips
- 1 cup chopped tomato
- ½ cup chopped red onion
- ⅓ cup tomato vegetable juice
- 2 tablespoons fresh lime juice
- ½ teaspoon ground cumin
- ½ cup chopped pecans, toasted
- Fresh parsley, for garnish

Heat 2 tablespoons oil in large skillet over medium heat until hot. Add chicken; stir-fry 2 minutes or until no longer pink in centers. Add garlic, jalapeño and ¾ teaspoon salt; stir-fry 30 seconds. Combine chicken mixture, lettuce, beans, cucumber, red pepper, tomato and onion in large salad bowl. Combine tomato juice, lime juice, remaining 2 tablespoons oil, cumin and remaining ½ teaspoon salt in small jar with lid; shake well. Place in skillet; heat over medium heat until slightly warm. Pour warm dressing over chicken mixture; toss to coat. Sprinkle with pecans. Garnish with parsley. Serve immediately.

Makes 4 servings

Favorite recipe from **National Broiler Council**

Fresh Fruity Chicken Salad

Yogurt Dressing (recipe follows)
2   **cups cubed cooked chicken**
1   **cup cantaloupe melon balls**
1   **cup honeydew melon cubes**
½   **cup chopped celery**
⅓   **cup cashews**
¼   **cup green onion slices**
      Lettuce leaves

Prepare Yogurt Dressing; set aside. Combine chicken, melons, celery, cashews and green onions in large bowl. Add dressing; mix lightly. Cover. Chill 1 hour. Serve on bed of lettuce.   *Makes 4 servings*

Yogurt Dressing

¼   **cup plain yogurt**
3   **tablespoons mayonnaise**
3   **tablespoons fresh lime juice**
¾   **teaspoon ground coriander**
½   **teaspoon salt**
      Dash of pepper

Combine ingredients in small bowl; mix well.

Makes about ½ cup

Paella Salad

Garlic Dressing (recipe follows)
2½ cups water
 1 cup uncooked rice
 1 teaspoon salt
 ¼ to ½ teaspoon powdered saffron
 2 cups cubed cooked chicken
 1 cup cooked deveined medium shrimp
  (about 4 ounces)
 1 cup diced cooked artichoke hearts
 ½ cup cooked peas
 2 tablespoons chopped salami
 2 tablespoons thinly sliced green onions
 2 tablespoons chopped drained pimiento
 1 tablespoon minced fresh parsley
  Lettuce or fresh spinach leaves
 1 large tomato, seeded and cubed, for
  garnish

Prepare Garlic Dressing; set aside.

Place water in 1-quart saucepan; heat to boiling. Stir
rice, salt and saffron into water. Reduce heat; cover and
simmer 20 minutes. Remove from heat; let stand until
water is absorbed, about 5 minutes. Refrigerate about
15 minutes.

Place rice, chicken, shrimp, artichoke hearts, peas,
salami, onions, pimiento and parsley in large bowl; toss
well. Pour dressing over salad; toss lightly to coat.
Cover and refrigerate 1 hour.

Arrange lettuce on large serving platter or 4 serving
plates; top with salad mixture. Garnish with cubed
tomato.   *Makes 4 to 6 servings*

Garlic Dressing

¾ cup olive or vegetable oil
¼ cup white wine vinegar
1 teaspoon salt
½ teaspoon pepper
1 clove garlic, pressed

Mix all ingredients in tightly covered jar.

Makes 1 cup

Note: Dressing can be refrigerated up to 2 weeks.

Warm Pork and Spinach Salad

1 pound boneless pork loin, cut into
  2×¼-inch strips
1 pound fresh spinach leaves, coarsely
  shredded
3 cups watercress sprigs
1 can (8 ounces) sliced water chestnuts,
  drained
1 cup thinly sliced celery
1 cup seedless green grapes
½ cup thinly sliced green onions
1 large Golden Delicious apple, cored and
  chopped
1 cup low-calorie Italian salad dressing
3 tablespoons light brown sugar
2 tablespoons dry white wine
2 tablespoons Dijon mustard
2 tablespoons toasted sesame seeds

Spray nonstick skillet with vegetable cooking spray;
stir-fry pork strips until cooked through, about 4
minutes. Set aside; keep warm. In large serving bowl,
toss spinach, watercress, water chestnuts, celery,
grapes, green onions and apple; toss to mix.

In small saucepan, combine salad dressing, brown
sugar, white wine and mustard; heat just until brown
sugar is dissolved, stirring constantly. Stir cooked pork
into hot dressing to coat well. Remove pork; pour half
of dressing over greens mixture in bowl; toss well.
Place pork strips on top of salad. Sprinkle with sesame
seeds. Pass remaining dressing.   *Makes 6 servings*

Favorite recipe from **National Pork Producers Council**

Crunchy Onion Layered Salad with Dilly Dijon Dressing

LAYERED SALAD

- 4 cups washed and torn salad greens
- 8 ounces boiled ham, cut into cubes
- 4 hard-cooked eggs, chopped
- 2 ripe tomatoes, chopped
- 1 bell pepper (green, red or yellow), seeded and chopped
- 1 bunch radishes, sliced
- 1 package (9 ounces) frozen peas, thawed and drained
- 1⅓ cups (2.8-ounce can) FRENCH'S® French Fried Onions

DILLY DIJON DRESSING

- 1 cup regular or reduced-fat mayonnaise
- 1 cup buttermilk or whole milk
- ¼ cup FRENCH'S® Dijon Mustard
- 1 package (1 ounce) ranch salad dressing mix
- ½ teaspoon dried dill weed

Layer salad ingredients in 3-quart straight-sided glass bowl. Combine Dilly Dijon Dressing ingredients in small bowl; mix well. Spoon onto salad just before serving. Garnish as desired.

Makes 4 main-dish or 6 side-dish servings
(about 2 cups dressing)

Gingered Pork Tenderloin Salad

 3 pounds pork tenderloin, thinly sliced
 ¼ cup teriyaki sauce
 3 tablespoons grated fresh ginger
 3 tablespoons chopped cilantro
 1 tablespoon cracked black pepper
 1 tablespoon olive oil
 12 artichoke hearts, quartered
 2 tablespoons butter
   Tangy Vinaigrette Dressing
     (recipe follows)
 6 red potatoes, boiled, peeled and sliced
 2 red onions, peeled and thinly sliced
   Lettuce leaves

Marinate pork slices in teriyaki, ginger, cilantro and pepper for 1 hour. Drain pork from marinade and stir-fry quickly in hot oil; set aside. Sauté artichoke pieces in butter until lightly browned. Prepare Tangy Vinaigrette Dressing. Toss pork, potatoes, artichokes and onions with dressing. Refrigerate. Arrange salad on lettuce-lined plates. Pass remaining dressing.

Makes 12 servings

Tangy Vinaigrette Dressing

1 cup olive oil
¾ cup rice vinegar
¼ cup chopped parsley
¼ cup chopped chives
3 anchovies, chopped
2 tablespoons chopped gherkins
1 tablespoon capers
2 cloves garlic, minced
2 teaspoons curry powder
Salt and pepper to taste

Combine all ingredients in small jar with tight-fitting lid. Shake well. *Makes about 2 cups*

Favorite recipe from **National Pork Producers Council**

Szechuan Pork Salad

½ pound boneless lean pork
4 tablespoons KIKKOMAN® Teriyaki
    Sauce, divided
⅛ to ¼ teaspoon crushed red pepper
1 cup water
2 tablespoons cornstarch
1 tablespoon distilled white vinegar
2 tablespoons vegetable oil, divided
1 onion, chunked and separated
12 radishes, thinly sliced
2 medium zucchini, cut into julienne
    strips
    Salt
4 cups shredded lettuce

Cut pork across grain into thin slices, then into narrow
strips. Combine pork, 1 tablespoon teriyaki sauce and
red pepper in small bowl; set aside. Combine water,
cornstarch, remaining 3 tablespoons teriyaki sauce and
vinegar; set aside. Heat 1 tablespoon oil in hot wok or
large skillet over high heat. Add pork; stir-fry 2
minutes; remove. Heat remaining 1 tablespoon oil in
same pan. Add onion; stir-fry 2 minutes. Add radishes
and zucchini; lightly sprinkle with salt. Stir-fry 1
minute longer. Stir in pork and teriyaki sauce mixture.
Cook and stir until mixture boils and thickens. Spoon
over bed of lettuce on serving platter; serve
immediately.   *Makes 2 to 3 servings*

Tuna Louie Salad

    Bibb lettuce
1 **can (12 ounces) STARKIST® Solid**
      White Tuna, drained and chunked
2 **avocados, sliced**
2 **to 4 hard-cooked eggs, sliced**
4 **plum tomatoes, sliced**
16 **ounces canned grapefruit sections,**
      drained and juice reserved
⅓ **cup whipping cream, whipped**
½ **cup Thousand Island dressing**
    Lime wedges

On four serving plates, arrange lettuce, tuna, avocados, eggs, tomatoes and grapefruit. In small bowl, fold whipped cream into Thousand Island dressing. For thinner dressing, add 1 to 2 tablespoons reserved grapefruit juice. Spoon dressing over salads or serve separately. Garnish with lime wedges.

Makes 4 servings

Tuna Pilaf Salad

1 package (7.2 ounces) RICE–A–RONI®
   Rice Pilaf
1 package (10 ounces) frozen cut green
   beans
1 small red onion, thinly sliced, slices
   halved
¼ cup Italian dressing
2 cans (6 ounces *each*) white tuna in
   water, drained, flaked
½ cup ripe pitted olives (optional)
1 large tomato, cut into 12 wedges
1 tablespoon chopped parsley

Prepare Rice-A-Roni Mix as package directs, reducing
water to 1¾ cups and stirring in frozen green beans and
onion during last 15 minutes of cooking.

Remove from heat; stir in dressing.

Top rice mixture with tuna, olives (if desired), tomato
and parsley.

Serve warm or chilled with additional dressing, if
desired. *Makes 5 servings*

StarKist® Salad Niçoise

¾ pound new red potatoes, cooked in their
    jackets, chilled and diced
1½ pounds fresh green beans, trimmed and
    blanched
8   sliced plum tomatoes *or* 1 pint cherry
    tomatoes, halved
¾ cup niçoise olives or halved ripe olives
½ cup thinly sliced red onion rings
3   tablespoons finely chopped Italian
    parsley
¾ teaspoon medium-grind black pepper
    Salt to taste
4   hard-cooked eggs, cut in quarters
1   can (12 ounces) STARKIST® Solid
    White Tuna, drained and chunked
1   cup bottled vinaigrette dressing, divided

On large platter, arrange all ingredients except
dressing. Cover with plastic wrap; chill. Just before
serving, drizzle about ½ cup dressing over all
ingredients; serve remaining dressing on side.

Makes 4 to 6 servings

Tip: Look for niçoise olives in gourmet section of
supermarket or in Italian deli.

Marinated Albacore and Mushroom Salad with Quick Sour Cream Dressing

1   can (6 ounces) STARKIST® Solid
    White Tuna, drained and chunked
1   pound mushrooms, cleaned and
    quartered
¼   cup chopped green onions, including
    tops
2   tablespoons minced fresh parsley
2   tablespoons lemon juice
2   teaspoons sugar
¼   teaspoon salt
¼   teaspoon white pepper
    Quick Sour Cream Dressing
    (recipe follows)
    Bibb lettuce
3   or 4 tomatoes, sliced or wedged, for
    garnish

In medium bowl, combine tuna, mushrooms, onions, parsley, lemon juice, sugar, salt and white pepper. Refrigerate, covered, 1 to 3 hours or until ready to serve. Just before serving, prepare Quick Sour Cream Dressing; fold into tuna mixture. Serve on lettuce-lined plates. Garnish with tomatoes.   *Makes 6 servings*

Quick Sour Cream Dressing

½ **cup whipping cream**
½ **teaspoon salt**
½ **teaspoon dry mustard**
¼ **cup sour cream**

In small bowl, beat whipping cream with salt and dry mustard until thickened; fold in sour cream.

Honey-Dijon Salad with Shrimp

8 **cups torn romaine lettuce leaves**
1 **pound large shrimp, cleaned and cooked**
3 **cups sliced mushrooms**
2 **cups sliced carrots**
½ **cup EGG BEATERS® Healthy Real Egg Product**
¼ **cup corn oil**
¼ **cup REGINA® White Wine Vinegar**
¼ **cup GREY POUPON® Dijon Mustard**
¼ **cup honey**
2 **cups plain croutons, optional**
   Carrot curls, for garnish

In large bowl, combine lettuce, shrimp, mushrooms and sliced carrots; set aside.

In small bowl, whisk together EGG BEATERS®, oil, vinegar, mustard and honey until well blended. To serve, pour dressing over salad, tossing until well coated. Top with croutons, if desired. Garnish with carrot curls.   *Makes 8 servings*

Warm Salmon Salad

Chive Vinaigrette (recipe follows)
2   cups water
¼   cup chopped onion
2   tablespoons red wine vinegar
¼   teaspoon black pepper
1¼ pounds small red potatoes
1   pound salmon steaks
6   cups torn washed mixed salad greens
2   medium tomatoes, cut into wedges
16 kalamata olives, sliced*

Prepare Chive Vinaigrette. Combine water, onion,
vinegar and pepper in large saucepan. Bring to a boil
over medium-high heat. Add potatoes. Cover and
simmer 10 minutes or until fork-tender. Using slotted
spoon, transfer potatoes to cutting board. Cool slightly.
Reserve water.

Cut potatoes into thick slices. Place in medium bowl.
Toss with ⅓ cup Chive Vinaigrette. Set aside.

Rinse salmon and pat dry with paper towels. Add fish to
reserved water. Over medium-high heat, bring water
just below a simmer. *Do not boil.* Adjust heat, if
necessary. Poach fish 4 to 5 minutes or until opaque
and fish flakes easily when tested with fork.

With slotted spoon, carefully remove fish from saucepan. Place on cutting board. Remove skin and bones from fish. Cut into 1-inch cubes.

Place salad greens onto 4 plates. Arrange fish, potatoes, tomatoes and olives on top. Drizzle with remaining Chive Vinaigrette.   *Makes 4 servings*

*Kalamata olives are imported from Greece and can be found at gourmet food specialty shops.

Chive Vinaigrette

⅓ **cup vegetable oil**
¼ **cup red wine vinegar**
2 **tablespoons finely chopped fresh chives**
2 **tablespoons finely chopped fresh parsley**
⅛ **teaspoon salt**
⅛ **teaspoon white pepper**

Combine all ingredients in jar with tight-fitting lid. Shake well to combine. Refrigerate.

Makes about ⅔ cup

Fruit

SALADS

Confetti Apple Salad

1 **Golden Delicious apple**
   (about 6 ounces), cored and chopped
½ **cup** *each* **flaked coconut, raisins and**
   chopped carrot
½ **cup lemon-flavored yogurt**
⅓ **cup coarsely chopped cashews or**
   peanuts
   Curly lettuce leaves

Combine all ingredients except nuts and lettuce and
allow flavors to blend for 1 hour. Stir in nuts. Arrange
salad on lettuce-lined plates.

Makes 2 to 3 servings

Favorite recipe from **Washington Apple Commission**

Apple Slaw with Poppy Seed Dressing

- 1 cup coarsely chopped unpeeled Jonathan apple
- 1 teaspoon lemon juice
- 2 tablespoons nonfat sour cream
- 1 tablespoon plus 1½ teaspoons skim milk
- 1 tablespoon frozen apple juice concentrate, thawed
- 1 teaspoon sugar
- ¾ teaspoon poppy seeds
- ½ cup sliced carrot
- ⅓ cup shredded green cabbage
- ⅓ cup shredded red cabbage
- 2 tablespoons finely chopped green bell pepper

Combine apple and lemon juice in resealable plastic food storage bag. Seal bag; turn to coat. Blend sour cream, milk, apple juice concentrate, sugar and poppy seeds in small bowl. Add apple mixture, carrot, cabbages and pepper; toss until well blended. Cover; refrigerate at least 1 hour before serving. Serve on cabbage leaves, if desired. *Makes 2 servings*

Four-Season Fruit Slaw

1 package (16 ounces) DOLE® Classic
    Cole Slaw
1 cup DOLE® Seedless Red or Green
    Grapes, halved
¾ cup DOLE® Chopped Dates or Pitted
    Prunes, chopped
⅓ cup sliced DOLE® Green Onions
¾ cup fat free or reduced fat mayonnaise
3 tablespoons apricot or peach fruit
    spread
½ cup DOLE® Slivered Almonds, toasted

• **Mix** cole slaw, grapes, dates and onions in large
serving bowl.

• **Stir** mayonnaise and fruit spread until blended in
small bowl. Spoon over cole slaw mixture; toss to
evenly coat. Cover.

• **Chill** 30 minutes. Stir in almonds just before serving.

Makes 6 servings

Basil Jicama Fruit Salad

1   cup *each* red and green California
        seedless grapes
1   cup cubed cantaloupe, honeydew melon
        or mango
1   cup fresh pineapple chunks
1   orange, peeled, sliced and quartered
1   nectarine, cubed
½   cup *each* halved strawberries and
        julienned jicama
¼   cup orange juice
1   tablespoon chopped fresh basil *or*
        1 teaspoon dried basil, crushed
    Orange-flavored yogurt, optional
    Basil sprigs, optional

Combine all ingredients except yogurt and basil sprig;
mix gently. Serve with dollop of yogurt and garnish
with sprig of basil, if desired.   *Makes 6 servings*

Favorite recipe from **California Table Grape Commission**

Fruit & Nut Salad

- 2 tablespoons low-calorie mayonnaise
- 1 tablespoon lemon juice
- 1 teaspoon honey
- ¼ teaspoon grated lemon peel
- 2 Golden Delicious apples, cored and cubed
- 1½ cups red or green seedless grapes
- 1 orange, peeled, sliced and chopped
- ½ cup chopped celery
- ½ cup chopped walnuts

In small bowl, whisk together mayonnaise, lemon juice, honey and lemon peel to make dressing. In large bowl, combine apples, grapes, orange, celery and walnuts; pour dressing over fruit mixture and toss to blend. *Makes 6 servings*

Favorite recipe from **Washington Apple Commission**

Anytime Fruit Salad

¼ cup vegetable oil

2 tablespoons fresh lime or lemon juice

2 teaspoons sugar

¼ teaspoon *each* black pepper and hot
   pepper sauce

1 medium tart apple, cut into thin wedges
   and halved

½ yellow bell pepper, cut into slices and
   halved

3 kiwi, peeled and sliced

½ cup *each* halved seedless red and green
   grapes

½ cup (2 ounces) coarsely chopped
   walnuts

1 cup (4 ounces) SARGENTO® Fancy
   Shredded Mild Cheddar Cheese
   Lettuce leaves

In small bowl, blend oil, lime juice, sugar, black pepper
and pepper sauce; set aside. In large bowl, combine
apple, bell pepper, kiwi, grapes and walnuts. Add lime
dressing; toss. Chill. Toss with Cheddar cheese. Serve
on lettuce-lined salad plates.   *Makes 6 servings*

Cool Summer Gazpacho Salad

1   DOLE® Fresh Pineapple
2   cups chopped tomatoes, drained
1   large cucumber, halved lengthwise and
     thinly sliced
¼   cup chopped DOLE® Green Onions
¼   cup red wine vinegar
4   teaspoons olive or vegetable oil
½   teaspoon dried basil leaves, crushed

• **Twist** crown from pineapple. Cut pineapple
lengthwise into quarters. Remove fruit from shell; core
and chop fruit. Drain.

• **Stir** pineapple, tomatoes, cucumber, green onions,
vinegar, oil and basil in large serving bowl; cover and
chill 1 hour or overnight. Stir before serving.

Makes 10 servings

Fruit Salad with Orange Poppy Seed Dressing

¼ cup orange juice

3 tablespoons cider vinegar

3 tablespoons FRENCH'S® Dijon Mustard

2 tablespoons honey

1 tablespoon FRENCH'S® Worcestershire Sauce

1 teaspoon grated orange peel

½ teaspoon salt

½ cup canola or corn oil

1 tablespoon poppy seeds

6 cups fruit, such as: orange segments; cantaloupe, watermelon and/or honeydew melon balls; blueberries; blackberries; grapes; star fruit and/or strawberry slices; nectarine wedges

Lettuce leaves

To prepare dressing, place juice, vinegar, mustard, honey, Worcestershire, orange peel and salt in blender or food processor. Cover and process until well blended. Gradually add oil in steady stream, processing until very smooth. Stir in poppy seeds. Arrange fruit on lettuce leaves on large platter. Spoon dressing over fruit just before serving.

Makes 6 side-dish servings
(about 1½ cups dressing)

The publishers would like to thank the companies and organizations listed below for the use of their recipes and photographs in this publication.

Alpine Lace Brands, Inc.
Best Foods, a Division of CPC International Inc.
Birds Eye
Bob Evans Farms®
California Table Grape Commission
California Tree Fruit Agreement
Christopher Ranch Garlic
Del Monte Corporation
Dole Food Company, Inc.
Filippo Berio Olive Oil
Golden Grain/Mission Pasta
Guiltless Gourmet, Incorporated
Hershey Foods Corporation
Hormel Foods Corporation
The HVR Company
Kahlúa Liqueur
Kellogg Company
Kikkoman International Inc.
Kraft Foods, Inc.
Lawry's® Foods, Inc.
McIlhenny Company
Nabisco, Inc.
National Broiler Council

National Fisheries Institute
National Foods, Inc.
National Honey Board
National Pork Producers Council
National Turkey Federation
Nestlé Food Company
New Jersey Department of Agriculture
Newman's Own, Inc.®
North Dakota Wheat Commission
Oscar Mayer Foods Corporation
The Procter & Gamble Company
Ralston Foods, Inc.
Reckitt & Colman, Inc.
Sargento® Foods Inc.
The Sugar Association, Inc.
Sunkist Growers
Surimi Seafood Education Center
USA Rice Council
Washington Apple Commission
Wisconsin Milk Marketing Board

312 Index

VOLUME MEASUREMENTS (dry)

⅛ teaspoon = 0.5 mL
¼ teaspoon = 1 mL
½ teaspoon = 2 mL
¾ teaspoon = 4 mL
1 teaspoon = 5 mL
1 tablespoon = 15 mL
2 tablespoons = 30 mL
¼ cup = 60 mL
⅓ cup = 75 mL
½ cup = 125 mL
⅔ cup = 150 mL
¾ cup = 175 mL
1 cup = 250 mL
2 cups = 1 pint = 500 mL
3 cups = 750 mL
4 cups = 1 quart = 1 L

VOLUME MEASUREMENTS (fluid)

1 fluid ounce (2 tablespoons) = 30 mL
4 fluid ounces (½ cup) = 125 mL
8 fluid ounces (1 cup) = 250 mL
12 fluid ounces (1½ cups) = 375 mL
16 fluid ounces (2 cups) = 500 mL

WEIGHTS (mass)

½ ounce = 15 g
1 ounce = 30 g
3 ounces = 90 g
4 ounces = 120 g
8 ounces = 225 g
10 ounces = 285 g
12 ounces = 360 g
16 ounces = 1 pound = 450 g

DIMENSIONS

1/16 inch = 2 mm
⅛ inch = 3 mm
¼ inch = 6 mm
½ inch = 1.5 cm
¾ inch = 2 cm
1 inch = 2.5 cm

OVEN TEMPERATURES

250°F = 120°C
275°F = 140°C
300°F = 150°C
325°F = 160°C
350°F = 180°C
375°F = 190°C
400°F = 200°C
425°F = 220°C
450°F = 230°C

BAKING PAN SIZES

Utensil	Size in Inches/ Quarts	Metric Volume	Size in Centimeters
Baking or Cake Pan (square or rectangular)	8×8×2	2 L	20×20×5
	9×9×2	2.5 L	23×23×5
	12×8×2	3 L	30×20×5
	13×9×2	3.5 L	33×23×5
Loaf Pan	8×4×3	1.5 L	20×10×7
	9×5×3	2 L	23×13×7
Round Layer Cake Pan	8×1½	1.2 L	20×4
	9×1½	1.5 L	23×4
Pie Plate	8×1¼	750 mL	20×3
	9×1¼	1 L	23×3
Baking Dish or Casserole	1 quart	1 L	—
	1½ quart	1.5 L	—
	2 quart	2 L	—